Questions and Answers

The Gospel of Matthew

Questions and Answers

The Gospel of Matthew
Mike Freze

BAKER BOOK HOUSE
Grand Rapids, Michigan 49516

Copyright 1987 by
Baker Book House Company

ISBN: 0-8010-3534-1

Printed in the United States of America

Contents

Preface   7

Before You Begin   9

1 Beginnings   11

2 The Twelve Disciples   29

3 Words of Jesus:
Sayings, Parables, Beatitudes   40

4 Teachings of Jesus:
Laws, Morals, Ethics   51

5 Miracles:
Visions, Healings, Appearances   60

6 The Spiritual World:
Angels, Demons, the Holy Spirit   70

7 Prophecy:
Old and New   81

8 Nature:
Earth, Animals, Air   91

9 The Passion   99

10 From Heaven Above:
God, Prayer, the Risen Christ   109

11 General Questions:
History, Archaeology, Geography, Unique Features   119

Answers   128

Preface

Many books deal with spiritual questions, are guides for building faith, or offer inspiration. However, I have been unable to find a book which has specific information from the Gospel of Matthew in question-and-answer form. When a wide variety of information—history, archaeology, geography, and literature—is gathered into one book, the result is a fascinating way to learn and also to understand more about the Gospel of Matthew.

Every Christian seems to feel that he or she knows something about Jesus' birth, his ministry, his passion, the disciples and their ministry, names and locations of familiar Bible places, and the people that were associated with our Lord's life on earth. But sometimes interesting details are forgotten or overlooked. These details often provide a meaningful background to Bible study.

In order to avoid the predictability of a sentence-by-sentence, question-and-answer format, I have randomly placed the questions under specific categories. This system avoids a book that resembles nothing more than a sequential commentary. Furthermore, this format makes it harder to memorize the answers.

Following the questions on the Gospel of Matthew itself is a general section on history, archaeology, geography, and unique features of the Gospels.

I hope you enjoy using the book as much as I enjoyed putting it together.

Mike Freze

Before You Begin

There are multiple choice options for each question throughout the book. The questions are designated:

> E —easy to answer
>
> M—moderately difficult
>
> H—difficult or hard to solve

Whether long or short, easy or hard, everyone has a 25-percent chance of answering each question correctly. Of course, the multiple choice option does not have to be used if one (or the group) knows the topic or category well.

The multiple choice options are short and specific. Several or all of the options may sound correct or reasonable but there is only one right answer for the question. Few obvious or silly choices are given to prevent the process of elimination from taking over.

Use the King James Version or the New International Version to verify your answers.

I hope you are ready now to challenge yourself in the fascinating world of information from the Gospel of Matthew. Enjoy!

Mike Freze

1

Beginnings

1. **M** Who was the father of Joseph (Mary's husband)?
   a. Eleazar   b. Zadok   c. Matthew   d. Jacob
2. **E** What did Joseph name Mary's child?
   a. Immanuel   b. Savior   c. Hosanna   d. Jesus
3. **H** According to Jesus' genealogy, Asa is the father of _____.
   a. Ram   b. Jehoshaphat   c. Obed   d. Josiah
4. **M** "Out of _____ I have called my son."
   a. Israel   b. Egypt   c. Jerusalem   d. bondage
5. **E** The angel said, "_____, son of David, have no fear about taking Mary as your wife."
   a. Jesse   b. Jesus   c. Joseph   d. John
6. **M** Why was King Herod angry at the Magi?
   a. They tricked him   b. He was jealous
   c. They attacked him   d. They stole his money
7. **E** Who came to King Herod, looking for a king whose birth was announced by a star?
   a. Magi   b. Shepherds   c. Prophets   d. Princes
8. **E** _____ was a preacher in the wilderness.
   a. James   b. Titus   c. John the Baptist   d. Simeon
9. **E** What did Joseph want to do when he found out that Mary was pregnant?
   a. Punish her   b. Marry her   c. Divorce her
   d. Leave town

10. **M** What does *Immanuel* mean?
    a. The anointed   b. God with us   c. Savior
    d. Blessed

11. **H** _____ is the son of Nahshon in Jesus' genealogy.
    a. Boaz   b. Salmon   c. Azor   d. Jesse

12. **M** Who opened their treasures and gave Jesus gifts?
    a. Herod's advisors   b. Simeon and Anna
    c. The Magi   d. Romans

13. **E** "Herod is searching for _____ to destroy him," said the angel.
    a. The Baptist   b. Philip   c. Titus   d. the child

14. **M** "We have observed his star at its _____."
    a. brightest   b. birth   c. peak   d. rising

15. **H** In Matthew's prologue, who is the father of Achim?
    a. Perez   b. Zadok   c. Nahshon   d. Abiud

16. **E** By whom did Mary become pregnant?
    a. Joseph   b. The Holy Spirit   c. David   d. Jacob

17. **M** When did Jesus, Mary, and Joseph leave Egypt?
    a. In the winter   b. When Herod died
    c. During Passover   d. The Bible doesn't say

18. **M** What other name did the prophets give to Jesus?
    a. The Chosen   b. God-bearer   c. Nazarene
    d. None of these

19. **H** In Jesus' genealogy, who is listed as Ram's grandfather?
    a. Perez   b. Salmon   c. Hezron   d. Boaz

20. **E** By which title did King Herod refer to the newborn Jesus?
    a. Messiah   b. Prophet   c. Savior   d. King

21. **M** _____ is the father of Jesse in Jesus' genealogy.
    a. Abraham   b. Ram   c. Obed   d. Jotham

22. **M** Archelaus succeeded his father Herod as king of _____.

    a. Perea   b. Judea   c. the Decapolis   d. Galilee

23. **E** John the Baptist made his appearance as a _____.

    a. preacher   b. healer   c. teacher   d. law-giver

24. **M** What story immediately follows Joseph's return to Nazareth?

    a. The ministry of John the Baptist
    b. King Herod's death   c. Jesus' childhood
    d. Jesus' temptation

25. **H** How many verses mention the Magi in Matthew? (chapter 2)

    a. 26   b. 3   c. 2   d. 10

26. **E** What were the Magi?

    a. Priests   b. Nomads   c. Astrologers   d. Kings

27. **E** What did John the Baptist wear around his waist?

    a. A cloak   b. A chain   c. A purse
    d. A leather belt

28. **H** _____ is the son of Joram in Jesus' genealogy.

    a. Uzziah   b. Boaz   c. Amminadab   d. Asa

29. **E** In which province does Matthew place Bethlehem?

    a. Galilee   b. Edom   c. Judea   d. Moab

30. **H** How many times is King Herod mentioned in Matthew? (chapter 2)

    a. 2   b. 9   c. 12   d. 24

31. **E** What event immediately follows the story of Jesus' birth?

    a. Jesus' genealogy   b. The visit of the Magi
    c. The census   d. The flight into Egypt

32. **M** John the Baptist ate _____ when he was in the wilderness.

   a. Cattle   b. Birds   c. Locusts and wild honey
   d. Roots and herbs

33. **H** _____ is the son of Perez in Jesus' genealogy.

   a. Hezron   b. David   c. Ahaz   d. Ram

34. **E** "Joseph, _____ of David, have no fear about taking Mary as your wife."

   a. son   b. lamb   c. grandson   d. heir

35. **M** From whom did King Herod find out where Jesus was to be born?

   a. Caesar   b. The Magi   c. Pilate
   d. Scribes and priests

36. **E** What name did the angel tell Joseph to give to the Savior?

   a. Christ   b. Jesus   c. Hosanna   d. Immanuel

37. **E** Why didn't the Magi return to Herod?

   a. They were warned in a dream   b. They got lost
   c. They left with Joseph   d. Herod died

38. **H** _____ is the father of Ahaz in Jesus' genealogy.

   a. Jesse   b. David   c. Jotham   d. Ram

39. **E** Who appeared to Joseph in a dream in Matthew's Gospel?

   a. An angel   b. God   c. Mary   d. The Holy Spirit

40. **H** Who does Matthew mention immediately after Amon?

   a. Hezekiah   b. Josiah   c. Jesus   d. Jesse

41. **M** Where did the slaying of children by King Herod occur, according to Old Testament prophecy?

   a. Bethlehem   b. Ramah   c. Near the Jordan
   d. Throughout all of Israel

42. E Who was the king of Judea when the wise men arrived?
   a. Augustus   b. Pilate   c. Herod   d. Tiberius
43. H In Matthew 1, who is the earliest ancestor of Jesus mentioned?
   a. Abraham   b. Moses   c. Jesse   d. Solomon
44. M Archelaus succeeded his father _____ as the king of Judea.
   a. Philip   b. Herod   c. Caesar   d. Pilate
45. M How did Jesus get his name?
   a. By Mary's request   b. Joseph chose it
   c. From an angel   d. By divine command
46. H How many mothers are mentioned between the generations of Abraham and Jesus?
   a. None   b. 2   c. 5   d. 12
47. E Who deceived Herod?
   a. His advisors   b. Simeon   c. The Magi
   d. Roman soldiers
48. H _____ is the father of Jotham in Jesus' genealogy.
   a. Uzziah   b. Zadok   c. Obed   d. Nahshon
49. M After returning from _____, Joseph went to the region of Galilee.
   a. Sidon   b. Syria   c. Egypt   d. Jerusalem
50. M What was Joseph called?
   a. Immanuel   b. Blessed Father
   c. Son of David   d. Josiah
51. M When did Jesus, Mary, and Joseph leave for Egypt?
   a. At night   b. Early morning   c. Midday   d. Dawn
52. E Where was Jesus born?
   a. Jerusalem   b. Nazareth   c. Bethlehem
   d. Galilee

53. **M** What did the Magi first do when they saw Mary and the child?
   a. They bowed down   b. They gave gifts
   c. They prayed   d. They sang

54. **H** _____ is the son of Amos in Jesus' genealogy.
   a. Boaz   b. Eliakim   c. Josiah   d. Judah

55. **H** In Jesus' genealogy, _____ is the father of Zadok.
   a. Ahaz   b. Jechoniah   c. Eliakim   d. Azor

56. **E** When did the wise men arrive in Jerusalem?
   a. After Jesus' birth   b. Before Jesus' birth
   c. After Herod died   d. Both a and c

57. **H** How many verses in Matthew suggest the virgin birth?
   a. 1   b. 2   c. 4   d. None

58. **E** Where were Mary and Joseph married?
   a. Nazareth   b. Bethlehem   c. Jerusalem
   d. Bethany

59. **H** In Matthew's prologue, who was Jesus' great-great-grandfather?
   a. Eleazar   b. Matthan   c. Eliud   d. Azor

60. **E** Who found Jesus with his mother Mary?
   a. Joseph   b. King Herod   c. Nicodemus
   d. The Magi

61. **M** How many times did angels speak to the Magi?
   a. Once   b. Twice   c. 3 times   d. None

62. **H** How many times is the word *Magi* mentioned in Matthew NIV?
   a. 16   b. 4   c. 1   d. 7

63. **M** How many times does Joseph speak in Matthew?
   a. 12   b. 36   c. 3   d. None

64. **H** What is the last word in the Gospel of Matthew?
    a. Peace   b. Christ   c. End   d. Age
65. **M** How did King Herod confront the Magi?
    a. Publicly   b. Secretly   c. He didn't
    d. Cautiously
66. **E** "The virgin shall be with _____."
    a. the Spirit   b. son   c. child   d. her people
67. **E** "Get up," said the angel, "take the _____ and his mother, and flee to Egypt."
    a. child   b. savior   c. colt   d. mule
68. **H** Who heard that King Herod was succeeded by Archelaus?
    a. Joseph   b. Mary   c. Philip   d. The Baptist
69. **H** In Matthew's prologue, who is the father of Hezron?
    a. Zerah   b. Ram   c. Jotham   d. Perez
70. **M** "The book of the generation of Jesus Christ, the son of _____, the son of Abraham."
    a. Jesse   b. Isaac   c. David   d. God
71. **E** Who was Mary's husband? (1:18)
    a. John   b. Joseph   c. David   d. Jacob
72. **M** What was Joseph's response to the angel's request?
    a. He disobeyed   b. He didn't believe
    c. He obeyed   d. He fainted
73. **E** John the Baptist's clothes were made of _____.
    a. goat skin   b. camel's hair   c. sheepskin
    d. horse hair
74. **M** Where else besides Bethlehem were children slain by King Herod?
    a. Areas around Bethlehem   b. Jerusalem
    c. Egypt   d. Nazareth

75. **E** Why did Joseph want to divorce Mary?
    a. Shame   b. God's command   c. Fear   d. a and c
76. **H** How many women are mentioned in Jesus' genealogy?
    a. 1   b. 2   c. 4   d. 5
77. **M** From the Babylonian captivity to the Messiah there are _____ generations.
    a. 6   b. 14   c. 24   d. 36
78. **M** After returning from Egypt, _____ went to the region of Galilee.
    a. Joseph   b. the astrologers   c. Herod   d. Simeon
79. **E** What three gifts were offered by the Magi to Jesus?
    a. Gold, frankincense, myrrh
    b. Silver, gold, bronze   c. Money, food, clothing
    d. Jewels, linen, perfume
80. **E** What title did the Magi give to Jesus?
    a. Savior   b. Messiah   c. King   d. Master
81. **M** In Matthew, what immediately follows John's baptism of Christ?
    a. Flight into Egypt   b. Healing
    c. The temptation   d. An exorcism
82. **H** The weeping and lamentation of Rachel for her children is the fulfillment of whose prophecy?
    a. Isaiah   b. Hosea   c. Jeremiah   d. Malachi
83. **H** In Jesus' genealogy, _____ is the father of Eliud.
    a. Achim   b. Tamar   c. Eleazar   d. Amos
84. **E** Who took his family to the land of Israel?
    a. Nicodemus   b. Astrologers   c. Scribes
    d. Joseph
85. **H** According to Jesus' genealogy, Salmon is the father of _____.
    a. Boaz   b. Asa   c. Ahaz   d. Solomon

86. M Who ruled Judea after King Herod died?
    a. Archelaus   b. Philip   c. Pilate   d. Josephus
87. E How is Joseph first identified in Matthew?
    a. As a carpenter   b. As a descendant of Adam
    c. As a religious man   d. As Mary's husband
88. M What is the first thing that Mary did in Matthew?
    a. She prayed   b. She became engaged
    c. She wept   d. She visited Elizabeth
89. H According to Jesus' genealogy, Amon is the father of _____.
    a. Jesse   b. Asa   c. Josiah   d. Hezekiah
90. E "Joseph, son of David, have no fear about taking Mary as your _____."
    a. prophetess   b. friend   c. wife   d. in-law
91. E Who was overjoyed at seeing a star?
    a. King Herod   b. Herod's advisors
    c. Astrologers   d. Joseph
92. M Where was Joseph afraid to go?
    a. Perea   b. Egypt   c. Galilee   d. Judea
93. H In Jesus' genealogy, _____ is the father of Eleazar.
    a. Eliud   b. Abijah   c. Matthan   d. Boaz
94. E Herod told the Magi to search diligently for the _____.
    a. Jews   b. child   c. priests   d. astrologers
95. H How many times in Matthew is Mary mentioned (without Joseph)?
    a. Once   b. Twice   c. 5 times   d. None
96. E Why was Joseph to name the child *Jesus*?
    a. He would be "the Anointed One"
    b. He would be righteous   c. He would save mankind   d. It was a common name

97. **H** In how many chapters does Matthew speak about Joseph?

 a. 1   b. 2   c. 3   d. 6

98. **M** How often does Matthew call the Magi "kings"? (chapters 1 and 2)

 a. Once   b. 3 times   c. All of the time   d. Never

99. **E** Who asked where the newborn king of the Jews was? (2:2)

 a. Astrologers   b. King Herod   c. Simeon   d. Joseph

100. **M** How many Marys are found in Matthew?

 a. 3 or 4   b. 6 or 8   c. 2   d. 13 or 14

101. **M** What happened to Joseph after he returned to Nazareth?

 a. He left Mary   b. He died   c. He became ill   d. It doesn't say

102. **M** _____ prophesied that John the Baptist would be "a voice of one calling in the wilderness."

 a. Isaiah   b. Malachi   c. Hosea   d. Ezekiel

103. **H** In Jesus' genealogy, _____ is the father of Shealtiel.

 a. Hezekiah   b. Jeconiah   c. Salmon   d. Tamar

104. **E** "The _____ shall be with child."

 a. Nazarene   b. barren   c. virgin   d. woman

105. **M** In Matthew's prologue, who is Jesus' grandfather?

 a. Matthan   b. Jesse   c. Eleazar   d. Jacob

106. **E** "_____ is searching for the child (Jesus) to destroy him."

 a. Judas   b. Ramah   c. Herod   d. Caesar

107. **H** In Matthew's prologue, who is the father of Jotham?

 a. Hezron   b. Perez   c. Uzziah   d. Josiah

108. E Of what marital status was Mary when she became pregnant?

a. Divorced   b. Married   c. Widowed   d. Engaged

109. E How did the angel address Joseph?

a. As the "son of David"
b. As a "master carpenter"   c. As a "saint"
d. Only as "Joseph"

110. M "The virgin shall be with _____."

a. child   b. son   c. king   d. savior

111. M What precedes the genealogy of Jesus in Matthew 1?

a. Creation   b. Solomon's reign   c. Moses
d. None of these

112. H In how many dreams did an angel appear to Joseph?

a. 1   b. 6   c. 3   d. 4

113. M People were being baptized by John in the river Jordan as they _____.

a. confessed their sins   b. cried out
c. shouted warnings   d. preached the gospel

114. E Who was afraid to go back to Judea?

a. Joseph   b. John the Baptist   c. An angel
d. Titus

115. H In Jesus' genealogy, _____ is the father of Jacob.

a. Zerah   b. Amos   c. Matthan   d. Hezekiah

116. E When Herod heard the wise men ask about the king of the Jews, he was _____.

a. troubled   b. overjoyed   c. sad   d. apathetic

117. M Where did Jesus, Mary, and Joseph go after leaving Egypt?

a. Judea   b. The Negev   c. Galilee   d. Jordan Rift

118. E What warning were the Magi given in a dream?

a. Go to Nazareth   b. Avoid Herod
c. Avoid Caesar   d. Keep silent

119. M In Matthew, which topic immediately precedes John's baptisms?

a. Jesus' birth   b. Jesus' return to Nazareth
c. Herod's election   d. The Census

120. E Who bowed down and worshiped Jesus when he was only a child?

a. The Magi   b. Enoch   c. King Herod
d. The Baptist

121. H What Old Testament prophet spoke of the children slain by King Herod?

a. Jeremiah   b. Daniel   c. Isaiah   d. Ezekiel

122. E What are the first verses in Matthew's gospel about?

a. Jesus' birth   b. Joseph and Mary
c. Jesus' genealogy   d. King Herod

123. E Joseph decided to divorce Mary _____.

a. quickly   b. quietly   c. in public   d. in court

124. E The famous astrologers in Matthew are also known as _____.

a. scribes   b. Magi   c. priests   d. Sanhedrin

125. E _____ said, "Go and get detailed information about the child."

a. Pilate   b. Herod   c. Caesar   d. The astrologers

126. M How many times does the word "virgin" refer to Mary in Matthew?

a. Once   b. 3 times   c. 8 times   d. None

127. H In Jesus' genealogy, _____ is the father of Zerubbabel.

a. Shealtiel   b. Ram   c. Manasseh   d. Asa

128. E "Joseph, son of David, have no _____ about taking Mary as your wife."

   a. fear   b. intentions   c. reservations   d. hope

129. E Astrologers asked Herod, "Where is the newborn _____?"

   a. king   b. Messiah   c. son   d. Nazarene

130. E In what town did Joseph settle after leaving Egypt?

   a. Nazareth   b. Bethlehem   c. Jerusalem   d. Capernaum

131. M According to Matthew, how many wise men were there?

   a. 3   b. 6   c. 12   d. It doesn't say

132. E Who was Jacob's father?

   a. Isaac   b. Abraham   c. David   d. Joseph

133. M The name *Immanuel* means, "_____ with us."

   a. God   b. the Savior   c. the Anointed One   d. the Son

134. H _____ is the Father of Amon in Jesus' genealogy.

   a. Obed   b. Manasseh   c. Hezekiah   d. Josiah

135. M When did Joseph respond to the angel's request?

   a. 1 week later   b. As soon as he woke up   c. After 3 days   d. 1 year later

136. M Who was Judah's father?

   a. Abraham   b. Perez   c. Jacob   d. Isaac

137. E Who received a message not to return to Herod?

   a. The Magi   b. Ramah   c. Mary   d. The Baptist

138. E Which topic immediately follows the genealogy of Jesus?

   a. Jesus' birth   b. John's birth   c. King Herod kills the infants   d. The astrologers seek Jesus

139. **E** Where did the wise men first go in Israel?
   a. Bethlehem   b. Jerusalem   c. Jericho
   d. Nazareth

140. **M** Where was the star when the Magi went to Bethlehem?
   a. Overhead   b. Behind them   c. Before them
   d. To the west

141. **H** By what name did the Old Testament prophet Micah refer to the newborn Christ?
   a. Christ   b. Ruler   c. Messiah   d. Savior

142. **M** According to Matthew, what did Joseph do for a living?
   a. Farming   b. Carpentry   c. Tent making
   d. It doesn't say

143. **E** Where did the wise men come from?
   a. The west   b. The east   c. Egypt   d. Heaven

144. **M** Who was told to name the Savior Jesus?
   a. Joseph   b. Mary   c. Elizabeth
   d. John the Baptist

145. **E** "Joseph, _____, have no fear about taking Mary as your wife."
   a. son of David   b. son of Jesse
   c. son of Abraham   d. father of Israel

146. **H** How many generations are there between Abraham and Christ?
   a. 37   b. 118   c. 42   d. 14

147. **E** How many descendants of Jesus are named in Matthew's genealogy?
   a. 24   b. None   c. 12   d. 40

148. **M** According to Old Testament prophecy, who was called out of Egypt?
    a. "The King"   b. "My Son" (Jesus)
    c. The Magi   d. Pharaoh

149. **E** "Joseph, son of _____, have no fear about taking Mary as your wife."
    a. Jesse   b. Abraham   c. Moses   d. David

150. **E** How old were the children slain by Herod?
    a. Under 1   b. 2   c. 1 month   d. 2 and under

151. **E** Who is Jesus' mother?
    a. Elizabeth   b. Ruth   c. Rahab   d. Mary

152. **M** According to Matthew, where did Mary go after Joseph found out about her pregnancy?
    a. Joseph's home   b. Elizabeth's home
    c. Her mother's home   d. Capernaum

153. **H** From the _____ to the time of Christ there are fourteen generations.
    a. seed of Jesse   b. Creation
    c. days of Solomon   d. Babylonian captivity

154. **M** _____ asked Herod, "Where is the newborn king?"
    a. Pilate   b. Caesar   c. The Magi   d. Archelaus

155. **E** _____ and wild honey were John the Baptist's food.
    a. Bees   b. Locusts   c. Oats   d. Wine

156. **M** "A family record of Jesus Christ, son of David, son of _____."
    a. Abraham   b. Jacob   c. Jesse   d. Moses

157. **E** What did Joseph decide to do when he heard about Mary's pregnancy?
    a. Divorce her   b. Separate   c. Marry her
    d. Marry someone else

158. H Which route did the Magi take to return home from Bethlehem?
a. Along the Jordan   b. Through Egypt
c. Across Arabia   d. Not known

159. E Where did the wise men first see the star of Christ?
a. Bethlehem   b. Jerusalem   c. In the east
d. In the west

160. E Jesus will save his people from their _____.
a. masters   b. sickness   c. sins   d. leaders

161. E "It is by the _____ that she [Mary] has conceived this child."
a. temple   b. Holy Spirit   c. prophecy
d. mercy of God

162. M What was the Savior's name to be, according to Isaiah?
a. Jesus   b. Son of man   c. Immanuel   d. Messiah

163. H How many times does Mary speak in Matthew?
a. Once   b. 2 times   c. 4 times   d. None

164. E What kind of man was Joseph?
a. Jealous   b. Sensitive   c. Righteous
d. It doesn't say

165. M Who said, "Get up, take the child and his mother, and flee to Egypt"?
a. King Herod   b. Simeon   c. An angel
d. John the Baptist

166. M "He shall be called a _____."
a. Nazarene   b. Judean   c. King   d. prophet

167. H After _____'s death, the angel of the Lord appeared in a dream to Joseph in Egypt.
a. Pilate   b. Caesar   c. Herod   d. Mary

168. **M** How often is Mary's father mentioned in Matthew?
a. Once   b. Twice   c. 3 times   d. Not once

169. **E** Who told Joseph to leave Israel?
a. Mary   b. The Magi   c. Zechariah   d. An angel

170. **M** What did the angel tell Joseph to do after King Herod died?
a. Stay in Egypt   b. Go to Israel   c. Pray   d. Rejoice

171. **E** Who said, "Go and get detailed information about the child"?
a. High priests   b. Astrologers
c. Pontius Pilate   d. King Herod

172. **M** In Matthew's prologue, who is Jesus' great-grandfather?
a. Jacob   b. Zadok   c. Matthan   d. Jesse

173. **E** John the Baptist made his appearance as a preacher in the wilderness of _____.
a. Galilee   b. Judea   c. Egypt   d. Syria

174. **H** According to the Old Testament prophecy about children King Herod would kill, who was weeping?
a. Rebecca   b. Mary   c. Rachel   d. Salome

175. **M** After returning from Egypt, Joseph went to the region of _____.
a. Judea   b. Idumea   c. Galilee   d. Perea

176. **E** "The kingdom of _____ is at hand!"
a. Christ   b. Jacob   c. David   d. heaven

177. **E** "A family record of _____, son of David, son of Abraham."
a. Solomon   b. Jesse   c. Moses   d. Jesus Christ

178. E Where did the star that the wise men followed stop?
    a. Above the place where Jesus was   b. Jerusalem
    c. Egypt   d. Above a pasture
179. H From the Babylonian captivity to the _____ there are fourteen generations.
    a. days of Titus   b. period of bondage
    c. time of Christ   d. reign of Caesar
180. E _____ will save people from their sins.
    a. The Father   b. Repentance   c. Confession
    d. Jesus
181. E "Herod is searching for the child to _____."
    a. pay him homage   b. worship him
    c. destroy him   d. question him
182. E "Where is the _____ king of the Jews?"
    a. risen   b. anointed   c. prophesied   d. newborn
183. M "Out of Egypt I have called my _____."
    a. savior   b. king   c. own   d. son
184. M Who made calculations about Jesus' age?
    a. Herod   b. Joseph   c. Ramah   d. The Zealots

2

The Twelve Disciples

1. **E** By which sea did Jesus call his first disciples?
   a. Mediterranean   b. Dead Sea   c. Galilee
   d. Huleh
2. **E** In Matthew, which disciple is mentioned first?
   a. Andrew   b. Simon   c. John   d. Bartholomew
3. **M** Besides his brother, who was with John when Jesus first called him?
   a. Simon   b. Zebedee   c. Andrew
   d. Bartholomew
4. **M** Which seasoning did Jesus compare his disciples to?
   a. Mustard seed   b. Sage   c. Pepper   d. Salt
5. **M** When Jesus calmed the storm, he said that the disciples were lacking in _____.
   a. faith   b. discipleship   c. teaching   d. healing
6. **E** Who saw Jesus eating with tax collectors, sinners, and the disciples?
   a. The Sadducees   b. Mary Magdalene
   c. Nicodemus   d. The Pharisees
7. **E** On which disciple did Jesus say he would build his church?
   a. Peter   b. John   c. Matthew   d. James

8. **M** Which disease did Jesus give the disciples the authority to cure?

   a. Blindness   b. Deafness   c. Leprosy
   d. Every kind

9. **E** To which disciple did Jesus reveal the beginnings of the church?

   a. James   b. John   c. Matthew   d. Peter

10. **M** Which disciple first spoke to Jesus as he walked on the water?

    a. John   b. Peter   c. James   d. Andrew

11. **H** In Matthew's list of the disciples, how many were called by more than one name?

    a. 1   b. 2   c. 3   d. None

12. **M** According to Jesus, the disciples were to be as innocent as _____.

    a. lambs   b. angels   c. sheep   d. doves

13. **E** Who helped Jesus feed the crowd of five thousand?

    a. John the Baptist   b. Part of the crowd
    c. The disciples   d. Nicodemus

14. **E** Which disciple walked on water toward Jesus?

    a. Peter   b. John   c. Matthew   d. None of them

15. **M** Where was Matthew when Jesus first called him?

    a. In his tax-collector's booth   b. At home
    c. Fishing   d. At John's house

16. **M** Who led the way to the boat on the Sea of Galilee?

    a. Peter   b. Jesus   c. Andrew   d. John

17. **E** What was Simon's (Peter's) trade?

    a. Tent maker   b. Tax collector   c. Fisherman
    d. Blacksmith

18. **M** Who was John's brother?
    a. James   b. Andrew   c. Matthew   d. Bartholomew
19. **E** Which disciple betrayed Jesus?
    a. Matthew   b. Simon   c. Thaddaeus
    d. Judas Iscariot
20. **H** Who was the fifth disciple that Jesus called?
    a. Judas Iscariot   b. Bartholomew   c. Matthew
    d. James
21. **E** Which relative of Peter's did Jesus cure of a fever?
    a. Sister   b. Mother-in-law   c. Father   d. Brother
22. **H** Where did Jesus tell Peter that he was a "Rock"?
    a. Cana   b. Caesarea Philippi   c. Capernaum
    d. Nazareth
23. **M** What did the Pharisees see the disciples doing on the Sabbath?
    a. Picking grain   b. Exorcisms   c. Praying
    d. Fishing
24. **H** At what time did Jesus walk on water toward the disciples?
    a. Mid-morning   b. Noon   c. Late afternoon
    d. Late at night
25. **E** Jesus called his disciples the _____ of the world.
    a. salt   b. light   c. seed   d. hope
26. **E** What did Peter's mother-in-law have?
    a. Demon possession   b. Leprosy
    c. Blindness   d. Fever
27. **E** What was Matthew's occupation?
    a. Scribe   b. Tax collector   c. Fisherman
    d. Shepherd

28. **M** What were Simon and Andrew doing when Jesus first called them?
   a. Fishing   b. Eating   c. Walking   d. Resting

29. **H** Exactly where was Peter when Jesus called him?
   a. On the shore   b. In Capernaum   c. In a boat
   d. It doesn't say

30. **M** Where did Jesus teach his disciples the Beatitudes?
   a. In Jerusalem   b. On a mountain
   c. By the seashore   d. In Capernaum

31. **M** Exactly where was John when Jesus first called him?
   a. On the shore   b. In a boat   c. In Capernaum
   d. It doesn't say

32. **E** How many disciples were named Simon?
   a. 1   b. 2   c. 3   d. None

33. **H** In Matthew's list of the disciples, which ones are mentioned with their father?
   a. James, John   b. John, James, Philip
   c. James, John, James   d. James, Thaddaeus

34. **E** Jesus rebuked _____ and the sea at Galilee.
   a. the rocks   b. the rain   c. the fog   d. the wind

35. **H** How did Jesus heal a relative of Peter's?
   a. By command   b. By prayer
   c. By touching her   d. With a glance

36. **M** How many disciples were named James?
   a. 1   b. 2   c. 3   d. None

37. **H** Which disciples buried John the Baptist?
   a. His own   b. Peter and James   c. Jesus'
   d. It doesn't say

38. **H** How many feet from shore was the disciples' boat when Jesus walked on the water?
    a. 10   b. 100   c. Several hundred
    d. It doesn't say

39. **E** The disciples were sent out as sheep among _____.
    a. men   b. goats   c. shepherds   d. wolves

40. **M** What did Jesus call Peter besides "Rock"?
    a. Son of Jonah   b. Son of David   c. Pope
    d. Simon the Just

41. **H** Where did the disciples land after Jesus walked on the water?
    a. Gennesaret   b. Cana   c. Sepphoris
    d. Capernaum

42. **H** Who was James's father?
    a. Theophilus   b. Thaddaeus   c. Alphaeus
    d. Zadok

43. **M** When speaking to his disciples about the harvest, Jesus referred to God as _____.
    a. the tenant   b. the Lord of the harvest
    c. the landlord   d. the workhorse

44. **E** What was Jesus doing when the storm came up on the Sea of Galilee?
    a. Sleeping   b. Praying   c. Fishing   d. Teaching

45. **M** Which disciple's house did Jesus visit?
    a. Andrew's   b. John's   c. Peter's   d. Matthew's

46. **E** What did Peter leave "at once" to follow Jesus?
    a. His wife   b. His brother   c. His boat   d. His net

47. **M** What theme immediately precedes the call of the first disciples?
    a. Evil   b. A wedding
    c. The kingdom of heaven   d. Discipleship

48. **M** Where were the disciples instructed not to go?
    a. Jerusalem   b. Any Samaritan town
    c. Any Galilean town   d. Any Gentile town

49. **E** In Matthew, where was the first place the disciples spoke to Jesus?
    a. Cana   b. Capernaum   c. The River Jordan
    d. The Sea of Galilee

50. **M** What kind of territory were the disciples told not to visit?
    a. Galilean   b. Desert   c. Pagan   d. Sanhedrin

51. **M** After Jesus walked on the water, what did the disciples call him?
    a. Master   b. Messiah   c. Lord   d. Son of God

52. **E** To which disciple did Jesus give the keys of heaven?
    a. Peter   b. John   c. Matthew   d. Judas

53. **E** Jesus called his disciples the _____ of the earth.
    a. light   b. seed   c. hope   d. salt

54. **H** In which chapter are all twelve disciples named?
    a. 2   b. 4   c. 8   d. 10

55. **M** The Pharisees asked the disciples about Jesus, referring to him as _____ .
    a. Son of David   b. the Messiah   c. Teacher
    d. Son of Joseph

56. **H** What did the Pharisees call the people Jesus ate with?
    a. Blasphemers   b. Sinners   c. Worms
    d. The lower class

57. **E** What was abandoned by Andrew immediately upon following Jesus?
    a. His brother   b. His net   c. His wife   d. His boat

58. E What was Andrew's trade?
    a. Tax collector   b. Tentmaker   c. Shepherd
    d. Fisherman
59. E Which disciples did Jesus call first?
    a. Simon, Andrew   b. Andrew, John
    c. John, Peter   d. Peter, James
60. M Besides his brother, who was with James when Jesus first called him?
    a. Zebedee   b. Andrew   c. Simon
    d. Bartholomew
61. H Near what territory did Jesus live when he called his first disciples?
    a. Zebulun   b. Naphtali   c. Both a and b
    d. Ammon
62. E Who was Andrew's brother?
    a. Bartholomew   b. Jesus   c. Simon   d. John
63. H In Matthew, how many disciples had been called when Jesus began teaching?
    a. 2   b. 4   c. 12   d. 13
64. H In Matthew's list of the disciples, which one is listed last?
    a. Bartholomew   b. Judas   c. Thaddaeus   d. Philip
65. M Which disciple was a Zealot?
    a. Simon   b. Thaddaeus   c. James   d. Philip
66. M In which disciple's home does Jesus first share a meal?
    a. Matthew's   b. John's   c. Peter's   d. James's
67. M What were the disciples supposed to do when they entered a good house?
    a. Give it their greeting   b. Wipe their feet
    c. Remove their shoes   d. Kiss the ground

68. H In Matthew, what is the first parable told to the disciples?

   a. The net   b. The seed   c. The weeds
   d. The mustard seed

69. E Whom did the disciples first think Jesus was when he walked on the water?

   a. An evil spirit   b. A sea monster   c. A ghost
   d. Elijah

70. H Which disciple was Alphaeus's son?

   a. Thaddaeus   b. Philip   c. John   d. James

71. M What was the first kind of authority that Jesus gave to the disciples?

   a. Exorcism   b. Prophecy   c. Teaching
   d. Discernment

72. M Whose disciples came to Jesus with a question?

   a. Peter's   b. John the Baptist's
   c. The Pharisees'   d. Herod's

73. E How many disciples did Jesus choose?

   a. 4   b. 6   c. 12   d. It doesn't say

74. E In Matthew's list of disciples, which one is listed first?

   a. Peter   b. John   c. James   d. Matthew

75. E How did Simon and Andrew respond when Jesus called them?

   a. They continued fishing   b. They laughed
   c. They doubted   d. They followed

76. M How did Jesus find the first two disciples?

   a. They approached him
   b. He saw them as he was walking
   c. Zebedee invited him   d. He had a vision

77. E What occupation did Jesus give to Andrew and Peter?
    a. Scribes   b. Great teachers
    c. Fishers of men   d. Priests

78. M Where was James when Jesus first called him?
    a. In a boat   b. On the shore   c. In Capernaum
    d. It doesn't say

79. E Who was the brother of James?
    a. Andrew   b. Zebedee   c. Simon   d. John

80. M What did John leave behind when Jesus called him?
    a. His boat   b. His net   c. His family   d. His catch

81. E Where was Andrew when Jesus called him?
    a. By the sea   b. Out at sea   c. In Capernaum
    d. It doesn't say

82. E What was Peter's original name?
    a. John   b. Peter   c. Petra   d. Simon

83. E Who was Simon's brother?
    a. Andrew   b. John   c. James   d. Bartholomew

84. H In Matthew, how many disciples have been listed when Jesus' teaching of the Beatitudes is recorded? (chapters 4 and 5)
    a. 2   b. 4   c. 10   d. 12

85. M Where was Jesus living when he called his first disciples?
    a. Nazareth   b. Cana   c. Capernaum
    d. Bethlehem

86. M In Matthew's list of the disciples, whose occupation is given?
    a. John's   b. James's   c. Matthew's   d. Peter's

87. **H** Whose disciples first asked Jesus about fasting?
 a. John's b. Matthew's c. Herod's d. Pilate's

88. **M** How many loaves of bread did Jesus multiply for the five thousand?
 a. 1 b. 5 c. 10 d. It doesn't say

89. **E** Besides preaching, curing the sick, and exorcisms, what other power did the disciples have?
 a. Multiplying bread b. Raising the dead
 c. Stopping sin d. Never dying

90. **M** Who was the father of James?
 a. Joses b. Theophilus c. Jesse d. Zebedee

91. **M** Who was John's father?
 a. Jesse b. Theophilus c. Zebedee d. Joses

92. **H** According to Jesus, the disciples were to be as shrewd as _____.
 a. owls b. snakes c. lions d. sheep

93. **M** Who were the third and fourth disciples that Jesus called?
 a. Bartholomew, Andrew b. James, Bartholomew
 c. James, John d. John, Andrew

94. **M** Where did Jesus go immediately after calling the first four disciples?
 a. Bethlehem b. The river Jordan
 c. Jerusalem d. Galilee

95. **E** Why did Peter sink into the Sea of Galilee?
 a. The boat collapsed b. The wind blew him
 c. He lacked faith d. He was sick.

96. **M** To whom were the disciples to minister first?
 a. The Jews b. The Samaritans
 c. The Gentiles d. Everyone

97. **M** Jesus lived by _____ when he called his disciples.
    a. a desert   b. water   c. a forest   d. plains

98. **M** What did James abandon when Jesus called him?
    a. His house   b. His net   c. His boat   d. His catch

99. **H** In Matthew's list of the disciples, who is the eleventh on the list?
    a. Simon the Zealot   b. Bartholomew   c. Philip   d. James

100. **E** What command did Jesus give to the disciples when he disclosed his messiahship?
    a. Tell the Sanhedrin   b. Tell the Gentiles
    c. Work miracles   d. Keep it secret

3

Words of Jesus
Sayings, Parables, Beatitudes

1. **M** To whom did Jesus say, "Permit it for now"?
    a. Peter and Andrew   b. Peter
    c. John the Baptist   d. Nicodemus
2. **E** Which disciples did Jesus speak to first?
    a. Peter and Andrew   b. James and John
    c. Philip and John   d. Peter and James
3. **E** What will the sorrowing be blessed with?
    a. Holiness   b. Consolation   c. Riches
    d. Good health
4. **M** In the parable of the seed, what does the good soil symbolize?
    a. Faith put to use   b. Heaven   c. Riches
    d. God's favor
5. **H** With what will the persecuted be blessed?
    a. The kingdom of heaven   b. Mercy
    c. Consolation   d. Holiness
6. **E** What parable talks about the buried treasure?
    a. The silver pieces   b. The hidden treasure
    c. The pearl   d. The yeast
7. **E** In the parable of the mustard seed, what becomes the largest plant?
    a. The fig tree   b. The vine
    c. The mustard plant   d. The wheat

8. **M** In the parable of the weeds, who came while everyone slept?
   a. An angel   b. An enemy   c. A nephew
   d. The wolves

9. **H** In which parable does a master leave his servants for a long time?
   a. The talents   b. The weeds
   c. The prodigal son   d. The treasure

10. **M** In which parable does a man sell all he has for land?
    a. The hidden treasure   b. The pearl
    c. The two sons   d. The yeast

11. **E** What word starts almost every Beatitude?
    a. God   b. Blessed   c. Mercy   d. Love

12. **H** Which parable claims, "The last shall be first and the first shall be last?"
    a. The weeds   b. The treasure   c. The vineyard
    d. The yeast

13. **E** In the parable of the vineyard, who paid the workmen?
    a. Jesus   b. The foreman   c. The slave
    d. The vineyard owner

14. **H** In the parable of the ten virgins, at what time did the groom arrive?
    a. Midnight   b. 6 p.m.   c. Noon   d. 6 a.m.

15. **E** Which parable talks about birds?
    a. The pearl   b. The seed   c. The two sons
    d. The mustard seed

16. **M** Where had Jesus been traveling before sharing the Beatitudes?
    a. Judea   b. Galilee   c. Perea   d. Idumea

17. **m** Who is the farmer growing good seed?
    a. Peter   b. A vinedresser   c. Zebedee
    d. The Son of man

18. **m** What is needed for good seed to grow?
    a. Soft soil   b. Herbs   c. Clear water   d. Good roots

19. **h** In the parable of the weeds, who asked to pull the weeds?
    a. A beggar   b. Servants   c. Jesus
    d. The landowner

20. **h** In the parable of the yeast, how many measures of flour were used?
    a. 1   b. 2   c. 3   d. 6

21. **e** In which parable are invitations cancelled?
    a. The prodigal son   b. Divine mercy
    c. The weeds   d. The wedding banquet

22. **h** Which is the shortest parable in Matthew?
    a. The weed   b. The mustard seed   c. The net
    d. The yeast

23. **m** How many times does Jesus speak to John the Baptist?
    a. Once   b. Twice   c. 3 times   d. Not once

24. **e** During his temptation, how often does Jesus refer to Scripture when confronting Satan?
    a. Once   b. Twice   c. 3 times   d. Not once

25. **m** How many Beatitudes are given in Matthew?
    a. 6   b. 8   c. 9   d. 12

26. **m** What will the merciful be blessed with?
    a. Consolation   b. Riches   c. Holiness   d. Mercy

27. **m** In the parable of the sower, who went out sowing?
    a. A farmer   b. A slave   c. A rich man
    d. A Samaritan

28. **H** In which parable does a person regret refusing to do something?

    a. The two sons   b. The prodigal son
    c. The tenants   d. The merciless official

29. **E** In the parable of the weeds, when will the wheat be divided from the weeds?

    a. Immediately   b. At harvest   c. In one week
    d. The end times

30. **M** In the parable of the seed, what made the seed wither?

    a. A flood   b. Hard soil   c. The sun   d. Insects

31. **H** Which parable has as its moral, "Keep your eyes open"?

    a. The ten virgins   b. Divine mercy
    c. The pearl   d. The prodigal son

32. **M** According to Jesus, why were the disciples' ears blessed?

    a. They are selective   b. They are prejudiced
    c. They hear   d. They are deaf

33. **E** From where did Jesus teach the Beatitudes?

    a. A lake   b. A mountainside   c. A river bank
    d. A mountain top

34. **H** In the parable of the talents, how much was earned on the two talents?

    a. Nothing   b. One talent   c. Two talents
    d. Five talents

35. **E** Which parable portrayed good being taken out of a lake?

    a. The treasure   b. The net   c. The pearl
    d. The silver pieces

36. **M** Which parable in Matthew comes first?

    a. The pearl   b. The seed   c. The net   d. The weed

37. **H** Which chapter in Matthew contains all of the Beatitudes?

   a. 1   b. 3   c. 5   d. 24

38. **M** In the parable of the seed, what can choke a planted seed?

   a. Worries   b. Wealth   c. The heat   d. Both a and b

39. **E** In the parable of the mustard seed, what is the seed compared to?

   a. Heavenly banquet   b. Kingdom of heaven
   c. Satan's dominion   d. Worldly kingdoms

40. **M** To whom does Jesus first speak with authority in Matthew?

   a. Peter   b. Satan   c. John the Baptist
   d. Nicodemus

41. **M** What will the poor in spirit be blessed with?

   a. Riches   b. Holiness   c. Consolation
   d. God's reign

42. **E** In the parable of the sower, how much can good seed yield?

   a. 30-fold   b. 60-fold   c. 100-fold   d. All of these

43. **M** What will the pure in heart be blessed with?

   a. God's land   b. Consolation   c. Seeing God
   d. Mercy

44. **H** In the parable of the yeast, who kneaded the dough?

   a. A woman   b. A child   c. An old man   d. An angel

45. **E** In the parable of the weeds, what was sown among the wheat?

   a. Barley   b. Oats   c. Weeds   d. Good seed

46. **E** In the parable of the mustard seed, what can be found in the branches?

   a. Birds   b. Weeds   c. Insects   d. Nothing

47. **M** In which parable does someone delay his coming?

   a. The ten virgins   b. The pearl   c. The tenants
   d. Divine mercy

48. **M** What is the field likened to in the parable of the weeds?

   a. Satan   b. The world   c. Jesus   d. Good citizens

49. **H** Which parable talks about saints?

   a. The weeds   b. The treasure
   c. The mustard seed   d. The wedding banquet

50. **M** In the parable of the two sons, which of the sons did what the father wanted?

   a. First   b. Second   c. Both   d. Neither

51. **H** In the parable of the ten virgins, how many virgins were foolish?

   a. 1   b. 2   c. 5   d. 10

52. **E** What is the good seed in the parable of the weeds?

   a. God's Word   b. The world
   c. Followers of Satan   d. Citizens of the kingdom

53. **E** Which parable involves a king's son?

   a. The tenants   b. The wedding banquet
   c. Divine mercy   d. The treasure

54. **H** What will the insulted be blessed with?

   a. A vision of God   b. Holiness   c. Consolation
   d. Reward in heaven

55. **H** Which parable in Matthew comes last?

   a. The net   b. Divine mercy   c. The talents
   d. The pearl

56. **E** In the parable of the weeds, where will the wheat be gathered?

   a. In a valley   b. In the plains   c. On a hill
   d. In a barn

57. **E** In the parable of the mustard seed, what starts as the smallest of seeds?

   a. A mustard plant   b. A vine   c. A weed
   d. A fig tree

58. **M** Whom does Jesus speak to first—Satan or the disciples?

   a. Satan   b. The disciples   c. Both
   d. Only 2 disciples

59. **E** What will Jesus make his disciples fishers of?

   a. Self   b. Wives   c. Men   d. Fish

60. **M** What will the meek be blessed with?

   a. The earth   b. Love   c. Heaven   d. Riches

61. **E** Where was Jesus most often when he spoke at length in parables?

   a. On a cliff   b. In a cave   c. In a boat
   d. In the towns

62. **M** In the parable of the sower, what does the seed on the path symbolize?

   a. The narrow gate   b. A wolf in sheep's clothing
   c. The message understood
   d. The message not understood

63. **H** What does the last Beatitude concern?

   a. Persecution   b. Poverty   c. Lowliness   d. Mercy

64. **M** In the parable of the weeds, what will happen to the weeds?

   a. They will burn   b. They will multiply
   c. They will be eaten   d. They will rot

65. **E** In the parable of the yeast, what is the kingdom of heaven like?

   a. Sugar   b. Flour   c. Flowing water   d. Yeast

66. H In which parable does oil play a key role?
   a. The sower   b. The leaven   c. The yeast
   d. The ten virgins
67. H In which parable is a tower erected?
   a. Divine mercy   b. The tenants   c. The pearl
   d. The prodigal son
68. H Which is Matthew's longest parable?
   a. The good Samaritan   b. Divine mercy
   c. The sower   d. The weeds
69. E Who sowed the weeds in the parable of the weeds?
   a. A sinner   b. The devil   c. The vinedresser
   d. Jesus
70. H Which Beatitude concerns meekness?
   a. First   b. Second   c. Third   d. Fifth
71. E Whom did Jesus call the "light of the world"?
   a. The Baptist   b. Lucifer   c. The Cherubim
   d. His disciples
72. M Which parable talks about fair wages?
   a. The two sons   b. The treasure
   c. The good Samaritan   d. The vineyard
73. H In the parable of the talents, how much did the "richest" servant have in the end?
   a. Two talents   b. five talents   c. Eleven talents
   d. Ten talents
74. M In the parable of the vineyard, how long did the last worker work?
   a. 1 hour   b. 3 hours   c. 6 hours   d. 10 hours
75. M Which parable says to forgive your brother from your heart?
   a. The good Samaritan   b. Divine mercy
   c. The unmerciful servant   d. The two sons

76. **M** Which parable speaks of forgiving seventy times seven?
    a. The two sons   b. The treasure
    c. The unmerciful servant   d. The tenants

77. **H** What does Jesus talk about first in Matthew's Gospel?
    a. Discipleship   b. God's demands
    c. Kingdom of heaven   d. The Spirit

78. **E** How many times does Jesus speak to Satan during the temptation?
    a. 1   b. 2   c. 3   d. 4

79. **E** According to Jesus, whom only may we worship?
    a. Himself   b. our neighbor   c. Mary
    d. God

80. **M** Where did Jesus first preach repentance?
    a. Jerusalem   b. The River Jordan   c. Nazareth
    d. Capernaum

81. **E** In the parable of the sower, what is the seed that fell on rock?
    a. Satan   b. A woman   c. A man   d. Jesus

82. **E** To whom does Jesus give the Beatitudes?
    a. Peter   b. A Samaritan   c. Mary Magdalene
    d. All of the disciples

83. **M** What theme is contained in the first Beatitude?
    a. Sorrow   b. Mercy   c. Poverty of spirit   d. Riches

84. **H** In the parable of the weeds, when did the weeds appear?
    a. When the crops died   b. When the slave died
    c. When the owner moved
    d. When the wheat matured

85. E In the parable of the weeds, what is the Kingdom of heaven compared to?
    a. A repentant man   b. A host of angels
    c. A man who sowed good seed   d. Jesus
86. M What will the peacemakers be blessed with?
    a. Holiness   b. Consolation   c. Mercy
    d. Being called sons of God
87. M In the parable of the net, who will separate the wicked from the just?
    a. The Father   b. The Son   c. Angels
    d. The apostles
88. H Which parable ends, "For many are called, but few are chosen?
    a. Divine mercy   b. The net
    c. The wedding banquet   d. The weeds
89. E On what besides bread is man to live?
    a. Water   b. Wine   c. The Spirit   d. God's word
90. E To whom did Jesus say, "You shall not put the Lord your God to the test"?
    a. Satan   b. Nicodemus   c. A Roman guard
    d. Judas
91. M What choked the seed in the parable of the sower?
    a. Sin   b. Water   c. Thorns   d. Insects
92. E What will the seekers of righteousness be blessed with?
    a. Consolation   b. They will be filled
    c. The Kingdom of heaven   d. Riches
93. M At his baptism, how does Jesus respond to John the Baptist's question?
    a. He agrees   b. He is silent   c. He is confused
    d. He disagrees

94. **H** Which parable claims, "You know not the day or the hour"?

    a. The weeds   b. The treasure
    c. The ten virgins   d. The mustard seed

95. **M** In the parable of the two sons, which son didn't work?

    a. The eldest   b. The youngest   c. Neither
    d. Both worked

96. **H** In the parable of the talents, how much in silver was to be entrusted to the servants?

    a. 5 talents   b. 7 talents   c. 8 talents   d. 10 talents

4

Teachings of Jesus
Laws, Morals, Ethics

1. **M** What did Jesus teach about first?
    a. Prayer   b. Death   c. Baptism   d. Discipleship
2. **E** "Treat others the way you would have them _____."
    a. treat themselves   b. behave   c. treat God
    d. treat you
3. **E** What should we do about our persecutors?
    a. Curse them   b. Agree with them
    c. Pray for them   d. Hate them
4. **E** How will false prophets appear to many people?
    a. In sheep's clothes   b. As angels   c. As Elijah
    d. As scholars
5. **E** "The harvest is good but the _____ are scarce."
    a. feeders   b. buyers   c. grains   d. laborers
6. **M** With what plant did Jesus compare strong faith?
    a. Manna   b. Rose   c. Mustard   d. Fig
7. **M** What must one do to be a brother or sister of Jesus?
    a. Repent   b. Good deeds   c. God's will
    d. Forgive
8. **E** "Give to Caesar what is _____."
    a. Caesar's   b. worthless   c. commanded
    d. valued

9. **H** According to Jesus, what Old Testament leader permitted divorce?
   a. Abraham   b. Moses   c. Jacob   d. Isaac

10. **E** "He who is not with me is _____."
    a. damned   b. against me   c. a lost sheep   d. the evil one

11. **M** To whom has the Father revealed what was once hidden?
    a. The scribes   b. The Baptist   c. Children   d. The Samaritan

12. **M** You cannot give yourself to God and _____.
    a. Satan   b. money   c. self   d. power

13. **H** To whom should we not give holy things?
    a. Dogs   b. Enemies   c. Nonbelievers   d. Sinners

14. **M** "Better to lose part of your body than to have it cast into _____."
    a. dust   b. clay   c. Gehenna   d. stone

15. **M** What is worth temporarily leaving the altar for?
    a. Reconciliation   b. Prayer   c. Burial   d. Baptism

16. **E** On what is man to live?
    a. Faith   b. God's Word   c. Living water   d. The Spirit

17. **M** What must men see as a result of the disciples' light?
    a. Good deeds   b. Faith   c. Fortitude   d. Suffering

18. **M** When should we appear clean and healthy?
    a. Before the altar   b. While fasting   c. While in prayer   d. In a crowd

19. **M** When a person strikes your right cheek, what should you do?
    a. Resist   b. Call the authorities   c. Strike him   d. Offer him the other cheek

20. E To what does Jesus compare the false prophets?
 a. Vultures b. Swine c. Wolves d. The scribes
21. E Where do man's evil designs come from?
 a. Evil friends b. The heart c. False prophets
 d. The body
22. M Who received the last teaching in Matthew?
 a. The Herodians b. The Sadducees
 c. The disciples d. The Samaritans
23. M Jesus came to bring _____ to the earth.
 a. division b. peace c. healing d. reconciliation
24. E Who is "Lord of the Sabbath"?
 a. The Son of Man b. The Spirit
 c. The high priest d. Adam
25. H What creatures did Jesus use to teach us about God's incomparable love for us?
 a. Sheep b. Wolves c. Colts d. Birds
26. E How many thrones will there be at the judgment?
 a. 1 b. 3 c. 12 d. 24
27. M According to Jesus, who in heaven is greater than John the Baptist?
 a. Children b. Martyrs c. Angels d. The least
28. E What kind of treasure should we store up for ourselves?
 a. Earthly b. Heavenly c. Universal d. Timeless
29. H If someone fails to settle with his adversary, to whom might he be handed over?
 a. Executioners b. The judge c. Jesus d. Satan
30. M Jesus compared the earth to what?
 a. God's footstool b. God's throne
 c. The saint's crown d. God's residence

31. E Jesus said, "Let _____ take care of itself."
   a. humanity   b. tomorrow   c. trouble
   d. the kingdom

32. H The _____ is the lamp of the body.
   a. spirit   b. soul   c. eye   d. flesh

33. E "Do not fear those who deprive the body but cannot destroy the _____."
   a. faith   b. mind   c. Spirit   d. soul

34. E Who really knows the Father?
   a. Children   b. The apostles   c. Jesus   d. No one

35. M What title did Jesus want the disciples to avoid?
   a. Prophet   b. Chosen ones   c. Rabbi   d. Scribe

36. E "Let no man separate what God has _____."
   a. joined   b. revealed   c. ordained   d. separated

37. M What must a man do to follow Jesus?
   a. Forgive   b. Deny himself   c. Pray
   d. Become baptized

38. M How often should we forgive someone who has sinned against us?
   a. 7 times   b. 70 times 7 times   c. 70 times
   d. Only once

39. E Who really knows the Son?
   a. Children   b. The apostles   c. All believers
   d. The Father only

40. E You can recognize a good tree by its _____.
   a. color   b. seed   c. fruit   d. branches

41. M The gate that leads to salvation is _____.
   a. wide   b. narrow   c. difficult   d. assured

42. E Jesus said, "Seek, and you will _____."
   a. perish   b. convert   c. find   d. believe

43. M "Where your treasure is, there your _____ will be also."

   a. heart   b. worth   c. reward   d. gain

44. H How far should we go when we are forced to go one mile?

   a. 1 mile   b. 2 miles   c. 10 miles   d. 20 miles

45. E Jesus said, "_____ your enemies."

   a. Love   b. Help   c. Resist   d. Ignore

46. H Where might one end up if differences aren't settled?

   a. In divorce   b. In prison   c. In loneliness
   d. In unbelief

47. H To whom were abusive speakers liable?

   a. The Sanhedrin   b. The rabbis
   c. Their friends   d. Their consciences

48. M What causes a woman to commit adultery?

   a. Lust   b. Pride   c. Marriage   d. Divorce

49. H To whom did Jesus quote Scripture regarding worship?

   a. Satan   b. John the Baptist   c. The Samaritan
   d. Peter

50. M Whom did Jesus teach first (according to Matthew's Gospel)?

   a. John the apostle   b. Satan   c. Peter
   d. John the Baptist

51. M Jesus instructed people to keep their deeds of mercy _____.

   a. simple   b. in obedience   c. secret   d. for God

52. E What must we seek first in order to acquire all of life's necessities?

   a. The kingdom   b. Humility   c. Repentance
   d. Baptism

53. **M** Whom will we know by their deeds?
    a. Demoniacs   b. False prophets   c. Angels
    d. Demons

54. **M** How many people will find the gate that leads to life?
    a. Everyone   b. Most people
    c. Half the people   d. Few

55. **M** What childlike condition should be imitated?
    a. Lowliness   b. Naivety   c. Innocence
    d. Truthfulness

56. **E** Many who are first shall _____.
    a. see God   b. believe   c. be first   d. be last

57. **H** Who had already come in Jesus' time to restore everything?
    a. Elijah   b. Enoch   c. The Spirit   d. Moses

58. **H** What will someday condemn us?
    a. Our words   b. Our deeds   c. Our conscience
    d. Our past

59. **E** To be worthy of Jesus, what must one take up?
    a. The Law   b. His sins   c. His cross   d. Nothing

60. **M** "No man can serve two _____."
    a. wives   b. laws   c. masters   d. gods

61. **M** What proves that we are sons of God?
    a. Laughter   b. Love for enemies   c. Money
    d. Friends

62. **H** What happens to our earthly treasures?
    a. They corrode   b. They get stolen
    c. Moths eat them   d. a, b, and c

63. **E** Where does swearing come from?
    a. Jealousy   b. Our minds   c. Adam   d. Satan

64. **H** Who was the second recipient of Jesus' teaching?
   a. Peter   b. Satan   c. James   d. Judas
65. **M** On what theme did Jesus first instruct the crowds?
   a. Love   b. Baptism   c. God's kingdom   d. Mercy
66. **M** "You are worth more than many _____."
   a. sheep   b. sparrows   c. angels   d. others
67. **E** Jesus said, "I have come to call _____."
   a. sinners   b. the faithful   c. the chosen
   d. the self-righteous
68. **H** What did Jesus tell his disciples to do if people persecuted them?
   a. Flee   b. Persevere   c. Convert them
   d. Curse them
69. **E** According to Jesus, who/what is "good"?
   a. Faith   b. Children   c. God   d. Life
70. **H** What derogatory name did Jesus call the Pharisees?
   a. Hypocrites   b. Thieves   c. Murderers   d. Fools
71. **M** How should we treat resolved differences following a quarrel?
   a. Tell everyone   b. Keep them secret
   c. Tell the priest   d. Be cautious
72. **M** What is an evil age always looking for?
   a. A sign   b. Revenge   c. The Messiah   d. Wealth
73. **E** If someone needs to borrow from us, what should we do?
   a. Charge interest   b. Use a contract
   c. Test him   d. Give freely
74. **E** "Offer no resistance to _____."
   a. false testimony   b. idolatry   c. injury   d. love
75. **H** To what did Jesus compare our need for clothing?
   a. Flowers   b. Sheep   c. Weeds   d. Birds

76. **H** What makes a man impure?
    a. His evil deeds   b. His body   c. His friends
    d. That which proceeds from his mouth

77. **M** Where will a blind man eventually lead another blind man?
    a. Toward sight   b. Toward God   c. Into a pit
    d. Toward mercy

78. **M** Who had nowhere to lay his head?
    a. Peter   b. John the Baptist   c. Jesus   d. Judas

79. **H** Jesus said, "It is mercy I desire and not _____."
    a. disbelief   b. suffering   c. pride   d. sacrifice

80. **H** Whom did Jesus remind about the sin of testing God?
    a. Judas   b. Peter   c. Joseph   d. Satan

81. **H** What did Jesus first talk to Peter about?
    a. Following him   b. Baptism   c. Heaven   d. Love

82. **M** Whoever welcomes a child welcomes _____.
    a. The elderly   b. his father   c. Jesus   d. his family

83. **E** What did Jesus say to do if one's right hand caused impurity?
    a. Hide it   b. Wash it   c. Burn it   d. Cut it off

84. **E** Besides the physical act, what else comprises adultery?
    a. Touching   b. Hearing about lust   c. Lusting
    d. Nothing

85. **E** Which Law was abolished when Jesus came?
    a. The first   b. The second   c. All of them   d. None

86. **M** Why should we not "swear by the earth"?
    a. It is Satan's   b. It is corrupt
    c. It is God's footstool   d. It is finite

87. E To what seasoning does Jesus liken the example of the disciples?

    a. Sugar   b. Wine   c. Salt   d. Yeast

88. E What does the Golden Rule sum up?

    a. Heaven   b. The parables   c. Judgment
    d. The Law and the Prophets

89. H What is a legitimate reason for divorce and remarriage?

    a. Unfaithfulness   b. Lying   c. Lack of love
    d. Deception

90. E "A man and wife shall become _____."

    a. like God   b. as angels   c. God's favored
    d. as one

91. M Those who publicize their good deeds are already _____.

    a. blessed   b. worthless   c. condemned   d. repaid

92. H Who will be least in God's kingdom?

    a. The boastful
    b. The adulterers and the divorced
    c. Those who sin and teach others to do the same
    d. The rich who do not tithe

93. H Who on earth should be called "father"?

    a. The scribe   b. The rabbi   c. The priest
    d. No one

94. M In New Testament times, who was the greatest man ever to be born besides Jesus?

    a. Peter   b. John the Baptist   c. Joseph   d. Adam

5

Miracles
Visions, Healings, Appearances

1. **H** What is the first miracle recorded in Matthew?
    a. Mary's pregnancy   b. Joseph's vision
    c. God's creation   d. John the Baptist's birth
2. **E** Where did Jesus cure Peter's mother-in-law?
    a. The synagogue   b. Peter's house
    c. John's house   d. By the sea
3. **H** What was the Canaanite's daughter cured of?
    a. Gluttony   b. Blindness   c. Leprosy
    d. Demon possession
4. **H** Where was the last place in Matthew that the risen Jesus appeared?
    a. Perea   b. The Decapolis   c. Galilee   d. Tyre
5. **M** Who said, "He (Jesus) casts out demons through the prince of demons"?
    a. The Sadducees   b. The Pharisees   c. Pilate
    d. Herod Antipas
6. **E** What miracle occurred while Jesus carried his cross?
    a. A physical healing   b. The Spirit appeared
    c. Jesus became transfigured   d. None
7. **E** The disciples could not cure _____ possessed by demons because they lacked faith.
    a. a boy   b. a baby girl   c. an old man
    d. an old woman

8. **H** In Matthew, where did the first miracle occur?
    a. Cana   b. Nazareth   c. Bethlehem
    d. It doesn't say

9. **H** Who received the first physical healing in Matthew?
    a. A deaf-mute   b. A blind man   c. A leper
    d. A retarded man

10. **E** Where did the resurrected saints appear?
    a. Capernaum   b. Jerusalem   c. Nazareth
    d. The River Jordan

11. **H** What miracle immediately follows the feeding of the five thousand?
    a. Changing water to wine   b. Walking on water
    c. A deaf-mute cured   d. A leper cured

12. **H** Where was the first blind man cured?
    a. Sidon   b. Jerusalem   c. Jericho   d. It doesn't say

13. **E** _____ was transfigured.
    a. Jesus   b. Enoch   c. Jacob   d. John

14. **M** Who was cured by touching Jesus' cloak?
    a. A woman   b. A priest   c. A boy   d. An old man

15. **M** How many of the disciples saw the risen Jesus in Galilee?
    a. 1   b. 2   c. 11   d. 12

16. **M** Whom did Jesus heal in the district of Tyre and Sidon?
    a. A Canaanite's daughter   b. A deaf-mute
    c. A blind man   d. A cripple

17. **E** Who was the first woman in Matthew to experience a miracle?
    a. Martha   b. Elizabeth   c. Anna   d. Mary

18. **E** Who appeared to Jesus during the temptation?
    a. God   b. Gabriel   c. Michael   d. Satan

19. **M** In Matthew, where did the first specific physical healing occur?

    a. In the river   b. By a lake   c. In a pool
    d. By a mountain

20. **M** To whom was the cured leper supposed to show himself?

    a. Pontius Pilate   b. A scribe   c. A priest
    d. Herod Antipas

21. **M** Who were the first to know about Jesus' resurrection?

    a. James and John   b. Peter and John
    c. Martha and Mary   d. Mary Magdalene and Mary

22. **M** What is the second miracle mentioned in Matthew?

    a. A shining star   b. A virgin birth
    c. An angelic visit   d. An exorcism

23. **E** What was the woman who touched Jesus' cloak cured of?

    a. Hemorrhages   b. Demonism   c. Leprosy
    d. Blindness

24. **E** Where did the disciples first see the risen Christ?

    a. Judea   b. Galilee   c. Idumea   d. Sidon

25. **M** Where did Jesus cure the two blind men?

    a. Cana   b. Bethany   c. Jerusalem   d. Jericho

26. **E** Where did the Spirit descend upon Jesus?

    a. The river Jordan   b. Bethsaida
    c. Gethsemane   d. Jerusalem

27. **H** Where was the Canaanite woman healed?

    a. Gilead   b. Judea   c. The Decapolis
    d. Tyre and Sidon

28. **E** Of what sickness did Jesus cure Peter's mother-in-law?

    a. Blindness   b. A fever   c. Leprosy   d. Deafness

29. **m** Who tried to plot against Jesus for restoring a shriveled hand?
    a. Caiaphas   b. Herod Antipas
    c. The Sadducees   d. The Pharisees

30. **h** What is the first healing miracle Jesus performed in Matthew?
    a. Curing the blind   b. Curing a leper
    c. Curing a deaf-mute   d. An exorcism

31. **e** In Matthew, who received the first vision of the Spirit?
    a. Simeon   b. Joseph   c. Mary   d. John the Baptist

32. **m** Where did Jesus heal the man with the shriveled hand?
    a. Martha's house   b. Peter's house
    c. The synagogue   d. The temple

33. **e** Who experienced the first miracle in Matthew?
    a. Joseph   b. John the Baptist   c. Simeon   d. Mary

34. **e** Who was ill and often fell into fire?
    a. A lunatic   b. A paralytic   c. An epileptic
    d. A blind man

35. **m** Who first heard a heavenly voice after Jesus' resurrection?
    a. The apostle John   b. Two women   c. Peter
    d. Martha

36. **m** Who was cured when Jesus said, "Out with you"?
    a. The men from the Gadarenes
    b. The centurion's servant   c. The leper
    d. The blind men

37. **h** Whose daughter did Jesus raise from the dead?
    a. A Samaritan's   b. The centurion's   c. Peter's
    d. A synagogue official's

38. **H** In Matthew, who received the first healing of any kind?
    a. A leper   b. A deaf-mute   c. A blind man
    d. A crippled man

39. **H** To whom did Jesus say, "I am willing. Be clean"?
    a. A blind man   b. A leper   c. A lunatic
    d. A deaf-mute

40. **E** Who rolled back the stone at Jesus' tomb?
    a. A Roman soldier   b. Elijah   c. An angel   d. Jesus

41. **M** How many people did Jesus feed first—four, five, or seven thousand?
    a. 4,000   b. 5,000   c. 7,000   d. It doesn't say

42. **H** Where was the first leper cured?
    a. Near a mountain   b. In the desert
    c. Jerusalem   d. Near the Sea of Galilee

43. **E** Who said, "Son of David, have pity on us"?
    a. Legion   b. Two blind men   c. Two lepers
    d. Three deaf-mutes

44. **E** Where was Jesus when he cured the centurion's servant?
    a. Nazareth   b. Tyre   c. Cana   d. Capernaum

45. **E** Who was the first to heal anyone in Matthew?
    a. Peter   b. Jesus   c. John the Baptist   d. Gabriel

46. **M** Who was the last in Matthew to see the risen Jesus?
    a. Nicodemus   b. Pontius Pilate   c. Martha
    d. All of the disciples

47. **E** Where did the virgin birth occur?
    a. Jerusalem   b. Bethlehem   c. Cana   d. Nazareth

48. **M** Who performed the first miracle in Matthew?
    a. The Son   b. The Father   c. The Spirit
    d. John the Baptist

49. **M** Whose heavenly appearance occurred first after the resurrection?

    a. Jesus'   b. The Spirit's   c. An angel's   d. Elijah's

50. **H** Whose daughter did Jesus heal at Tyre?

    a. A Sadducee's   b. A Canaanite's   c. A Syrian's   d. An Idumean's

51. **E** Who appeared in the first vision in Matthew?

    a. Enoch   b. Elijah   c. God   d. An angel

52. **E** Which miracle in Matthew was the first to fulfill an Old Testament prophecy?

    a. A healing   b. The resurrection
    c. The crucifixion   d. The virgin birth

53. **E** Where did Jesus rebuke water?

    a. The Mediterranean   b. The Dead Sea
    c. The Sea of Galilee   d. The river Jordan

54. **M** Where did the first healing occur?

    a. Syria   b. Idumea   c. Judea   d. It doesn't say

55. **M** What did the angel's appearance at Jesus' tomb resemble?

    a. Lightning   b. A cloud   c. The Spirit   d. Jesus

56. **H** Where did Jesus go after the feeding of the four thousand?

    a. Magadan   b. Perea   c. Sidon   d. The Decapolis

57. **M** Who was the second person in Matthew to experience a miracle?

    a. Jesus   b. Mary   c. Joseph   d. John the Baptist

58. **M** What did Jesus touch in order to cure Peter's mother-in-law?

    a. Her hand   b. Her face   c. Her leg   d. Her eyes

59. **H** In Matthew, who cried out to Jesus for mercy?

    a. The Greek   b. The Roman   c. The Samaritan
    d. The Canaanite

60. **H** Who was cured when Jesus said, "Courage, daughter"?
    a. A blind child   b. A bleeding woman
    c. A leper   d. A deaf woman

61. **M** At Jesus' death, who was raised from the dead?
    a. John the Baptist   b. Elijah   c. Lazarus   d. Saints

62. **M** Who was cured when Jesus forgave his sins?
    a. A demoniac   b. A deaf-mute   c. A paralytic
    d. A lunatic

63. **E** What did Jesus touch in order to cure the two blind men?
    a. Their hands   b. Their faces   c. Their eyes
    d. Nothing

64. **H** Who was the second person that Jesus cured?
    a. Mary Magdalene   b. A lunatic
    c. Peter's mother   d. The centurion's servant

65. **E** Who was cured when Jesus said, "Go home"?
    a. A demoniac   b. A deaf-mute   c. Martha
    d. The centurion's servant

66. **E** Who received the first vision in Matthew?
    a. Mary   b. Joseph   c. John the Baptist   d. Peter

67. **H** Who said, "Lord, if you are willing, you can make me clean"?
    a. A leper   b. A blind man   c. A demoniac
    d. A paralyzed man

68. **H** How long had the four thousand been with Jesus before he fed them?
    a. 1 day   b. 2 days   c. 3 days   d. 1 week

69. **M** From what was the centurion's servant cured?
    a. Paralysis   b. Demon possession
    c. Blindness   d. Deafness

70. **E** What kind of healing required prayer and fasting?
    a. Restoration of sight   b. Restoration of hearing
    c. An exorcism   d. None
71. **E** What type of ailments did Jesus cure early in his ministry?
    a. Demon possession   b. Lunacy   c. Paralysis
    d. All of these
72. **M** Who received the first exorcism in Matthew?
    a. Martha   b. Mary Magdalene
    c. The Gadarene men   d. The centurion's servant
73. **H** Whom did Jesus heal in the synagogue after leaving the grainfields?
    a. A blind man   b. A deformed man
    c. A demoniac   d. A leper
74. **H** Who was the last (according to Matthew) to be addressed by the risen Jesus?
    a. Joseph of Arimathea   b. Nicodemus   c. Peter
    d. His disciples
75. **E** What miracle did Pontius Pilate experience?
    a. An exorcism   b. A physical healing
    c. A heavenly vision   d. None
76. **M** What Old Testament prophet's predicted miracle was first to be mentioned in Matthew?
    a. Jeremiah   b. Obadiah   c. Isaiah   d. Moses
77. **E** Who felt he was not worthy to have Jesus enter his home in order to cure someone?
    a. Nicodemus   b. The centurion   c. Simeon
    d. A leper
78. **M** Whom did Jesus cure at Jericho?
    a. A paralytic   b. A leper   c. Two blind men
    d. No one

79. E Who said about Jesus, "He has been raised, exactly as promised"?
    a. An angel   b. Jesus   c. Elijah   d. Nicodemus

80. E Whose mother-in-law did Jesus cure?
    a. Philip's   b. James's   c. Peter's   d. Bartholomew's

81. M Who was the first non-Jew to experience a miracle in Matthew?
    a. King Herod   b. The centurion's servant
    c. Pontius Pilate   d. Nicodemus

82. E Who was the first man in Matthew to experience the supernatural?
    a. John the Baptist   b. Joseph   c. Simeon   d. Jesse

83. E Who first informed Mary Magdalene of Jesus' resurrection?
    a. An angel   b. Peter   c. Martha   d. James and John

84. E What miracle led the centurion to call Jesus the "Son of God"?
    a. Darkness   b. A heavenly voice
    c. An earthquake   d. A storm

85. H Who was the first cured person told by Jesus to remain quiet?
    a. A blind man   b. A demoniac   c. A leper
    d. A lunatic

86. E On what day did Jesus restore a shriveled hand?
    a. The Sabbath   b. Passover
    c. The Feast of Tabernacles   d. The first day of Jubilee

87. E Where did the angel sit when he came to Jesus' tomb?
    a. In the tomb   b. On a hill   c. On a cloud
    d. On a stone

88. **E** Lord, _____, have pity on me!"
   a. Messiah   b. Son of David   c. my Savior
   d. my God

89. **E** In Matthew, what is the first miracle performed by God the Father?
   a. A flood   b. An exorcism   c. A healing
   d. The descending Spirit

90. **M** What miracle immediately precedes Jesus' walking on the water?
   a. Feeding of the five thousand
   b. A demoniac cured   c. A leper cured
   d. A mute cured

91. **M** After a miracle, who said, "Clearly this was the Son of God"?
   a. Peter   b. John   c. Martha   d. The centurion

92. **H** What instrument was played as Jesus went to cure a deaf girl?
   a. Trumpet   b. Drum   c. Flute   d. Horn

93. **H** About whose cure did people say, "Nothing like this has ever been seen in Israel"?
   a. A blind man's   b. A bleeding woman's
   c. A leper's   d. A mute's

94. **H** How long had the woman hemorrhaged before Jesus cured her?
   a. 1 year   b. 7 years   c. 12 years   d. 20 years

95. **M** In Matthew, where did the first exorcism occur?
   a. Nazareth   b. Cana   c. Bethany
   d. The region of the Gadarenes

96. **M** Where did Joseph receive his first vision?
   a. The River Jordan   b. Nazareth   c. Bethlehem
   d. It doesn't say.

6

The Spiritual World
Angels, Demons, the Holy Spirit

1. **E** Who told Mary and Joseph not to go to Judea?
   a. An angel   c. Satan   c. The Spirit   d. Caiaphas
2. **E** Where did the Spirit of God that descended upon Jesus "as a dove" come from?
   a. The waters   b. The heavens   c. The clouds
   d. The sun
3. **E** How long did Jesus fast before his temptation?
   a. 4 days and nights   b. 2 weeks
   c. 40 days and nights   d. 2 months
4. **M** How many of the possessed brought to him did Jesus cure?
   a. Very few   b. About half   c. Most   d. All of them
5. **E** To what did the Pharisees attribute Jesus' power of exorcism?
   a. God   b. Astrologers   c. Hypnosis   d. Satan
6. **H** From where will the angels gather God's chosen in the last days?
   a. The four winds   b. All lands   c. The clouds
   d. The seas
7. **H** What is the blessing for the poor in spirit?
   a. Consolation   b. Kingdom of heaven   c. Mercy
   d. Seeing God

8. **H** Jesus says that Capernaum will not be "exalted to heaven." Where will it go?

   a. The evil garden   b. To Hades
   c. A burning furnace   d. Into the sea

9. **E** Jesus once said to Peter, "Get out of my sight, you _____!"

   a. hypocrite   b. evil one   c. Satan   d. doubter

10. **M** Which of the angels in heaven is married?

    a. Raphael   b. Gabriel   c. The cherubim   d. None

11. **M** What will the gates of hell not be able to prevail against?

    a. The Ten Commandments   b. The church
    c. Mankind   d. Peter

12. **E** What did the Gadarene demons enter into after being expelled?

    a. Other people   b. Mules   c. Swine   d. Hell

13. **E** According to Jesus, with what will some people exorcise demons?

    a. Confidence   b. The Holy Spirit
    c. Discernment   d. Jesus' name

14. **H** Whose Old Testament prophecy was repeated by an angel in Joseph's dream?

    a. Isaiah's   b. Malachi's   c. Baruch's   d. Amos's

15. **M** What happened immediately after Jesus was baptized?

    a. Satan was expelled   b. The sky opened
    c. A man's blindness was cured
    d. The earth shook

16. **E** What part of the Lord's Prayer mentions the evil one?

    a. The beginning   b. The middle   c. The end
    d. No part

17. **M** With what did Satan tempt Jesus while on the mountain?

   a. Control of nature   b. The world's kingdoms
   c. Eternal happiness   d. Everlasting life

18. **E** At Jesus' baptism, how did the Spirit of God participate?

   a. It lifted him   b. It subdued him
   c. It entered him   d. It hovered over him

19. **E** Jesus once said, "Get behind me, _____!"

   a. brothers   b. Pharisees   c. daughters   d. Satan

20. **M** What message did the angel at Jesus' tomb want conveyed?

   a. Satan is defeated   b. Christ has risen
   c. The Spirit will come   d. Pilate has defected

21. **H** Whose exorcism resulted in the claim by the Pharisees that Jesus cast out demons by the power of Satan?

   a. A dumb man's   b. A paralytic's   c. A leper's
   d. A blind man's

22. **H** What is the first parable in Matthew to mention angels?

   a. The mustard seed   b. The weeds
   c. The leaven   d. The pearl

23. **E** Besides prayer, what was needed for the disciples to cure the possessed boy?

   a. Touching   b. Fasting   c. Discernment
   d. The gift of healing

24. **H** In what type of towns were the apostles forbidden to cast out demons?

   a. Samaritan   b. Roman   c. Philistine   d. Greek

25. E What kind of spirit did the disciples think they saw on the Sea of Galilee?
    a. Evil spirit   b. A ghost   c. An angel   d. The Holy Spirit

26. M To whom is the Holy Spirit first revealed in Matthew?
    a. Jesus   b. Mary   c. Zechariah   d. Joseph

27. E In the region of the Gadarenes, from where did the possessed men come to confront Jesus?
    a. Homes   b. The sea   c. Hell   d. Tombs

28. M Whom did the angel speak to at the tomb of the risen Jesus?
    a. The two Marys   b. Nicodemus
    c. A Roman guard   d. Joseph of Arimathea

29. H Where did the demons confront Jesus about the "appointed time"?
    a. Bethsaida   b. Bethany
    c. The region of the Gadarenes   d. Tyre

30. M How many times did angels warn Mary and Joseph of danger?
    a. Once   b. Twice   c. 3 times   d. Not once

31. E How many times did Satan tempt Jesus in the wilderness?
    a. Once   b. Twice   c. 3 times   d. 4 times

32. M To whom did the angel first give commands?
    a. Joseph   b. Mary   c. Elizabeth   d. Jesus

33. M What were the people from the region of the Gadarenes afraid to do because of demons?
    a. Enter their homes   b. Befriend someone
    c. Pass by a certain way   d. Pray

34. **M** According to Jesus, what will grind "in the darkness"?
    a. Teeth   b. Axes   c. Hot stones   d. Bones
35. **E** Who "sows the weeds"?
    a. The Pharisees   b. The angels   c. Sinners
    d. Satan
36. **E** Who will accompany Jesus at his second coming?
    a. Angels   b. The Father   c. The Holy Spirit
    d. No one
37. **M** What country does the angel mention by name to Joseph?
    a. Egypt   b. Israel   c. a and b   d. None
38. **E** Who cured the possessed boy with a harsh command?
    a. Jesus   b. Peter   c. The centurion   d. John
39. **M** To whom did Jesus first give authority to expel demons?
    a. Peter   b. All twelve disciples
    c. The Pharisees   d. The priests
40. **H** How many men possessed by demons did Jesus cure in the region of the Gadarenes?
    a. 1   b. 2   c. 12   d. 24
41. **E** Who revealed the Spirit to Joseph?
    a. An angel   b. Satan   c. The Father
    d. It doesn't say
42. **E** With what did John say Jesus would baptize?
    a. Water   b. Oil   c. Water and oil
    d. The Holy Spirit
43. **M** In what district did Jesus first perform exorcisms?
    a. Judea   b. Galilee   c. Idumea   d. The Decapolis

44. **H** From where did Satan want Jesus to jump?
    a. A cliff   b. A crevasse   c. A tall house
    d. The temple
45. **E** Who led Jesus to the place of temptation?
    a. A demon   b. Satan   c. The Holy Spirit
    d. John the Baptist
46. **E** What crime against the Holy Spirit can never be forgiven?
    a. Forgetfulness   b. Confusion   c. Doubt
    d. Blasphemy
47. **M** Where did the demon-infested swine ultimately end up?
    a. The sea   b. The desert   c. A cave   d. A crevasse
48. **E** "The _____ is willing but nature is weak," said Jesus.
    a. Lord   b. mind   c. spirit   d. good
49. **H** Where did Jesus heal the Canaanite woman's daughter?
    a. The district of Tyre and Sidon   b. Bethsaida
    c. Capernaum   d. The region of the Gadarenes
50. **H** From whom were the apostles to expel demons first?
    a. The Jews   b. The Samaritans   c. The Romans
    d. All of the Gentiles
51. **M** Over what issue did Jesus once refer to Peter as a devil?
    a. The crucifixion   b. The resurrection
    c. Temptation   d. Both a and b
52. **H** Which is mentioned first in Matthew?
    a. An angel   b. The Holy Spirit   c. Satan
    d. John the Baptist

53. **H** In the parable of the weeds, who are the harvesters?
    a. Angels   b. Saints   c. The poor   d. Human souls
54. **E** How did Jesus usually expel demons?
    a. By prayer   b. By touching   c. With a word
    d. With a stare
55. **E** How did the demon-infested swine die?
    a. Burning   b. Drowning   c. Suffocation
    d. Energy loss
56. **M** How many times did an angel appear to Joseph in Egypt?
    a. Once   b. Twice   c. 3 times   d. Not once
57. **E** Where did Jesus want John to baptize him?
    a. In the River Jordan   b. Jerusalem   c. Emmaus
    d. In the Sea of Galilee
58. **M** "The spirit is willing but _____ is weak."
    a. the mind   b. our conscience   c. the flesh
    d. our will
59. **E** What did Satan command Jesus to miraculously change?
    a. A stone   b. A hill   c. A wall   d. Money
60. **E** What did Satan want Jesus to do in order to gain all the kingdoms of the world?
    a. Hate him   b. Forgive him   c. Worship him
    d. Forget him
61. **E** By whom did Jesus want to be baptized?
    a. The Father   b. John the Baptist   c. An angel
    d. Peter
62. **M** Who would help the disciples speak in court trials and synagogues?
    a. Nicodemus   b. The scribes
    c. The Holy Spirit   d. Themselves

63. **H** According to Jesus, how many spirits may re-enter a previously-possessed man if he's careless?
    a. 1   b. 7   c. 12   d. None

64. **E** What has been prepared for Satan and his angels?
    a. Eternal thirst   b. Every disease
    c. Punishing angels   d. Everlasting fire

65. **M** To whom will the spirit of Christ proclaim justice?
    a. The Gentiles   b. The Jews   c. The dead
    d. The widowed

66. **M** What did the disciples need in order to cure the possessed boy?
    a. Approval of Jesus   b. The Holy Spirit
    c. Trust   d. Authority

67. **H** When was Joseph supposed to leave Egypt?
    a. At the angel's command   b. During Passover
    c. During the Sabbath   d. At daybreak

68. **E** Who said, "Satan cannot expel Satan"?
    a. Jesus   b. Satan   c. Peter   d. Nicodemus

69. **E** What happened when Jesus died?
    a. The earth shook   b. Tombs were opened
    c. The veil of the temple was torn
    d. All of these

70. **E** Which disciple did Jesus once call "Satan"?
    a. John   b. Thomas   c. Peter   d. James

71. **E** Jesus said to Peter, "Get out of my _____, you Satan!"
    a. sight   b. life   c. kingdom   d. mind

72. **M** Who first revealed the name of Jesus?
    a. Mary   b. Joseph   c. An angel   d. The Holy Spirit

73. **H** What caused the first angel to appear in Matthew?
    a. Infidelity   b. Intended marriage   c. Travel
    d. Intended divorce

74. **M** Who first announced Jesus' baptism?
    a. John the Baptist   b. An angel   c. The Father
    d. Simeon

75. **E** Who came to Jesus immediately after Satan's temptations?
    a. Angels   b. John the Baptist   c. Mary
    d. Mary Magdalene

76. **E** What human need did Satan first capitalize upon when he tempted Jesus?
    a. Money   b. Clothing   c. Love   d. Food

77. **E** Who tempted Jesus in the desert?
    a. Satan   b. King Herod   c. The Holy Spirit
    d. No one

78. **H** How often does Matthew mention the name "Gabriel"?
    a. Once   b. Twice   c. 3 times   d. Not once

79. **M** By what other name did Jesus frequently refer to hell?
    a. Underworld   b. The abode   c. Gehenna
    d. The abyss

80. **E** Who encouraged Mary and Joseph to go to Egypt?
    a. The Father   b. The Spirit   c. Satan   d. An angel

81. **M** Which of the angels knows the exact time of the second coming?
    a. Gabriel   b. Michael   c. Raphael
    d. None of them

82. **H** Who constantly sees the heavenly Father's face?
    a. The lowly   b. The saints   c. The prophets
    d. The angels

83. **H** "Better to lose part of your body than to have it cast into _____."
    a. Gehenna   b. Darkness   c. Confusion
    d. The abyss

84. **H** By what other name did the Pharisees identify Satan?
    a. Prince of darkness   b. Baal   c. Beelzebub
    d. Lucifer

85. **H** Where did the possessed boy whom the disciples could not cure frequently fall?
    a. Onto sharp rocks   b. Into deep sleep
    c. Into temptation   d. Into fire

86. **M** Whom did Satan say would protect Jesus through his trials?
    a. The apostles   b. God   c. Angels   d. Himself

87. **E** When will the Holy Spirit reveal the time of the second coming?
    a. In 1 generation   b. In 3 generations   c. Soon
    d. Never

88. **H** According to Jesus, who will hurl evildoers into hell?
    a. Jesus   b. The Holy Spirit   c. The Father
    d. Angels

89. **H** Where did demons first address Jesus as "Son of God"?
    a. The suburbs of Capernaum
    b. The region of the Gadarenes
    c. Jericho   d. Near Jerusalem

90. **E** What did Jesus do just before he died?
    a. He cursed Satan   b. He drank wine
    c. He pondered   d. He cried out

91. **M** Beelzebub is the _____ of demons.
    a. king   b. master   c. prince   d. lord

92. **M** By what other proper name does Jesus call Satan?

a. Hana   b. Beelzebub   c. Baal   d. Gormah

93. **H** In the parable of the net, who separates the wicked from the just?

a. Jesus   b. The Father   c. The Holy Spirit
d. The angels

94. **M** Where did some demons enter into a herd of swine?

a. Jerusalem   b. The region of the Gadarenes
c. Jericho   d. Cana

95. **E** What will dispatch the angels from heaven at the second coming?

a. Bells   b. A trumpet   c. Winds   d. A choir

96. **M** To which city did Satan lead Jesus while tempting him?

a. Bethlehem   b. Jerusalem   c. Jericho   d. Bethany

7

Prophecy
Old and New

1. **H** Who is the main subject of the first prophecy in Matthew?
   a. Adam   b. Jesus   c. Abraham
   d. John the Baptist
2. **M** Which town is the subject of the second prophecy in Matthew?
   a. Bethlehem   b. Jerusalem   c. Nazareth   d. Nain
3. **E** "In the last days, there will be weeping and gnashing of _____."
   a. Wheat   b. Axes   c. Teeth   d. Stone
4. **E** Whom did Isaiah call "a voice in the desert"?
   a. Jesus   b. Satan   c. Gabriel   d. John the Baptist
5. **H** Which Old Testament prophet gave the Nazarene prophecy?
   a. Micah   b. Obadiah   c. Isaiah   d. Not known
6. **E** To whom in Matthew's Gospel does the "preparation" prophecy refer?
   a. John the Baptist   b. David   c. King Herod
   d. Mary
7. **M** "Hosanna to the Son of _____."
   a. Israel   b. God   c. Abraham   d. David

8. **M** Who will accompany Jesus at his second coming?

   a. The patriarchs   b. Angels   c. The apostles
   d. No one

9. **E** Who will appear in the end times to deceive many people?

   a. The Jews   b. Demons   c. Satan
   d. False prophets

10. **H** What New Testament city did Jesus prophetically condemn?

    a. Capernaum   b. Bethsaida   c. Chorazin
    d. All of these

11. **E** "Where the carcass lies, there the _____ gather."

    a. demons   b. vultures   c. snakes   d. sinners

12. **E** Whom did Jesus say would betray him?

    a. Peter   b. Judas   c. Satan   d. Pilate

13. **H** In Matthew, which prophet first calls Jesus *shepherd*?

    a. Micah   b. Ezekiel   c. Moses   d. Hosea

14. **M** Who received the first prophetic message in Matthew?

    a. Joseph   b. Mary   c. John the Baptist
    d. The wise men

15. **E** Who or what was the recipient of Jesus' curse?

    a. The Gentiles   b. Cana   c. A fig tree
    d. The Samaritans

16. **H** To which prophet does Jesus refer regarding washing hands before eating?

    a. Obadiah   b. Daniel   c. Isaiah   d. Moses

17. **M** In Matthew, who said, "The virgin shall be with child"?

    a. Daniel   b. Jeremiah   c. Isaiah   d. Moses

18. **H** Which Old Testament prophet did the wise men quote?

    a. Micah   b. Nehemiah   c. Hosea   d. Jeremiah

19. **E** "Heaven and earth shall pass away, but my _____ will not pass away."

    a. power   b. words   c. love   d. kingdom

20. **M** "Do not think that I (Jesus) have come to abolish the law and the _____."

    a. prophets   b. Scripture   c. scribes   d. Gentiles

21. **H** Whose prophecy was fulfilled by the slaughter of the infants?

    a. Micah's   b. Jeremiah's   c. Isaiah's   d. Sirach's

22. **E** Which prophet said, "It was our infirmities he (Jesus) bore"?

    a. Hosea   b. Micah   c. Malachi   d. Isaiah

23. **M** "If you are prepared to accept it, he (the Baptist) is _____."

    a. Moses   b. Enoch   c. Elijah   d. Jacob

24. **H** From which Old Testament book did Jesus quote when he said, "I will speak in parables"?

    a. Isaiah   b. Psalms   c. Sirach   d. Deuteronomy

25. **M** Jesus prophesied his second coming and indicated that his people will be hated by all nations for _____.

    a. His name's sake   b. their victorious battles
    c. their faith   d. their chosen status

26. **H** From which prophet did Jesus quote when he said, "I will strike the shepherd"?

    a. Zechariah   b. Ezekiel   c. Isaiah   d. Jeremiah

27. **M** In the end times, what will be darkened?

    a. The sun   b. The stars   c. The moon   d. a and c

28. **H** From which Old Testament book does Jesus borrow his second retort to Satan?

   a. Exodus   b. Leviticus   c. Joshua   d. Deuteromony

29. **M** Who will share the heavenly banquet with God?

   a. The rabbis   b. The patriarchs   c. The kings
   d. The prophets

30. **E** "Blessed is he who comes in the name of _____."

   a. the Spirit   b. the Lord   c. God's people
   d. the Messiah

31. **E** "You will hear of _____ and rumors of _____."

   a. death   b. signs   c. wars   d. betrayal

32. **E** "You shall not put the Lord your God to the _____."

   a. Pharisees   b. wolves   c. flesh   d. test

33. **E** "He shall be called a _____."

   a. new seed   b. carpenter   c. shepherd
   d. Nazarene

34. **M** To whom did the wise men quote an Old Testament prophecy?

   a. John the Baptist   b. Joseph   c. King Herod
   d. Jesus

35. **H** How many prophecies in Matthew have no known source?

   a. 1   b. 2   c. 3   d. None

36. **M** In Matthew, to whom did Jesus first quote Scripture?

   a. Satan   b. John the Baptist   c. His mother
   d. Joseph

37. **H** Which Old Testament book claimed, "Blessed is he who comes in the name of the Lord"?

   a. Hosea   b. Psalms   c. Deuteronomy   d. Proverbs

38. E To whom did Jesus first talk about his tragic death?
    a. The disciples   b. John the Baptist
    c. Mary Magdalene   d. Pontius Pilate
39. H "In his (Jesus) name, the _____ will find hope."
    a. Jews   b. Romans   c. sinners   d. Gentiles
40. E "The kingdom of _____ is at hand."
    a. Heaven   b. Satan   c. Israel   d. Caesar
41. E Isaiah prophesied, "And they shall call him _____."
    a. Righteous One   b. Immanuel   c. King
    d. Messiah
42. M How many times does Jesus quote Old Testament Scripture to Satan in the desert?
    a. Once   b. Twice   c. 3 times   d. Not once
43. H Whose prophecy did Mary and Joseph fulfill by leaving Egypt?
    a. Micah's   b. Hosea's   c. Isaiah's   d. Moses'
44. H Which prophet did Jesus quote from to reprimand the money changers?
    a. Obadiah   b. Moses   c. Daniel   d. Isaiah
45. E If not on bread alone, on what shall man live?
    a. Manna   b. God's Word   c. Wheat   d. Water
46. M Where was the "cry" of Jeremiah's prophecy heard?
    a. Ramah   b. Jerusalem   c. In all of Israel   d. Egypt
47. M Who quoted, "He will bid his angels take care of you"?
    a. John the Baptist   b. Peter   c. Satan   d. James
48. E What is the prophetic equivalent for "God is with us"?
    a. Christ   b. Savior   c. Messiah   d. Immanuel

49. M In the last days, what will fall from the sky?
   a. The sun   b. The moon   c. The stars
   d. The planets

50. E How was the first prophecy in Matthew transmitted?
   a. Through the Spirit   b. Through prayer
   c. Through Jesus   d. Through a dream

51. H "Land of _____, land of Naphtali, along the sea beyond the Jordan."
   a. Tyre   b. Zebulum   c. Sidon   d. Judea

52. M Who said that people should not worry about food or drink?
   a. Joseph   b. John the Baptist   c. Jesus   d. Hosea

53. E "Know that I am with you always, even until _____."
   a. death   b. the end of the age
   c. my resurrection   d. the Sabbath

54. M In the last days, who will blow the trumpet?
   a. Jesus   b. The angels   c. The apostles
   d. The Father

55. E "Out of _____ I have called my son."
   a. heaven   b. Bethlehem   c. Egypt   d. glory

56. M What is the first town mentioned in the prophecies in Matthew?
   a. Jerusalem   b. Bethlehem   c. Jericho   d. Cana

57. M Why did an angel first speak in Matthew?
   a. To announce an engagement
   b. To bring a divine command   c. To rebuke Satan
   d. To participate in a baptism

58. E "Can you not read the signs of the _____?"
   a. Pharisees   b. Prophets   c. Spirit   d. Times

59. **M** Where should people in Judea flee when they see the abomination of desolation"?
    a. To the mountains   b. To the desert
    c. To Egypt   d. To cellars
60. **E** "Hosanna in the _____."
    a. highest   b. Chosen Land   c. kingdom   d. Spirit
61. **M** Whose prophecy did John the Baptist appear to fulfill?
    a. Jeremiah's   b. Micah's   c. Isaiah's   d. Hosea's
62. **M** Whom does Matthew say spoke through the prophet Isaiah?
    a. Jesus   b. John the Baptist   c. The Lord
    d. Moses
63. **E** Who will know the exact time of Jesus' return?
    a. The Father   b. Jesus   c. The angels   d. No one
64. **H** At Jesus' return, what will the Savior place on his left?
    a. Sheep   b. Vultures   c. Swine   d. Goats
65. **E** About whose evil deed was Jeremiah's "massacre" prophecy?
    a. All of Israel   b. Pontius Pilate   c. King Herod
    d. Judas Iscariot
66. **H** By moving to Capernaum, whose prophecy did Jesus fulfill?
    a. Isaiah's   b. Hosea's   c. Ezekiel's   d. Jeremiah's
67. **E** "Prepare the way of the _____."
    a. Savior   b. Lord   c. Messiah   d. Christ
68. **E** To whom did Jesus talk about the destruction of the temple?
    a. The disciples   b. The Sadducees
    c. King Herod   d. Pontius Pilate

69. **M** After which of the following will the end of time finally come?
    a. Wars   b. Satan's victory
    c. Gospel proclamation   d. Disease

70. **E** "My house shall be called a house of _____."
    a. faith   b. prayer   c. love   d. hope

71. **M** In Matthew, what woman is named in Jeremiah's prophecy?
    a. Mary   b. Sarah   c. Rebecca   d. Rachel

72. **M** History has not known a man born of woman greater than _____.
    a. Moses   b. Jesus   c. John the Baptist   d. Peter

73. **E** "The Son of Man is coming at a time you _____."
    a. Long for him   b. Know from prophecy
    c. Repent   d. Least expect

74. **H** Jeremiah's prophecy was in reference to what?
    a. The lineage of Jesus   b. Herod's massacre
    c. Jesus' birth   d. Egypt

75. **E** Who first confronted Jesus about his predicted crucifixion?
    a. John the Baptist   b. The apostle John
    c. Peter   d. Philip

76. **E** Jesus said, "Nation will rise against _____."
    a. nation   b. God   c. cities   d. the kingdom

77. **M** For whose sake will the days of God's wrath be shortened?
    a. The apostles   b. The chosen people
    c. The children   d. All sinners

78. **E** To which Old Testament figure does Jesus refer when speaking of doomsday?
    a. Noah   b. Abraham   c. Moses   d. Jezebel

79. **E** In which chapter of Matthew is a prophecy first quoted?

 a. 1   b. 2   c. 4   d. 5

80. **M** Which Old Testament prophet called Jesus "Immanuel"?

 a. Daniel   b. Jeremiah   c. Isaiah   d. Moses

81. **E** The teachers of the law told King Herod that the Christ was to be born in Bethlehem of _____.

 a. the chosen land   b. Galilee   c. Jesse   d. Judea

82. **H** Which chapter and verse of Isaiah prophesied the virgin birth?

 a. 1:1   b. 4:7   c. 7:14   d. 12:4

83. **M** At Jesus' return, who will be placed at his right hand?

 a. Sheep   b. Angels   c. Repentant sinners
 d. His mother

84. **M** Which prophet said, "Our sufferings he (Jesus) endured"?

 a. Obadiah   b. Isaiah   c. Jeremiah   d. Hosea

85. **M** In Matthew, who quoted Micah's prophecy?

 a. An angel   b. Joseph   c. The wise men
 d. King Herod

86. **E** Which Old Testament prophet is mentioned first in Matthew?

 a. Isaiah   b. Daniel   c. Moses   d. Ezekiel

87. **E** Who quoted the first prophecy in Matthew?

 a. Joseph   b. Mary   c. An angel   d. The Father

88. **H** From which Old Testament book does Jesus quote in his third answer to Satan?

 a. Deuteronomy   b. Exodus   c. Judges   d. Genesis

89. M Where did the disciples ask Jesus about the end of the world?

a. Gethsemane b. Mount Tabor c. The temple
d. The Mount of Olives

90. E Which prophet spoke of the coming "abomination of desolation"?

a. Isaiah b. Daniel c. Jeremiah d. Ezekiel

91. M "I assure you, _____ has already come, but they did not recognize him."

a. Moses b. Enoch c. Elijah d. the Baptist

92. E "This people pays me _____ service."

a. poor b. lip c. selfish d. wicked

93. H Which Old Testament book does Jesus quote from first?

a. Genesis b. Exodus c. Deuteronomy
d. Leviticus

94. E What are the "birth pangs" of Jesus' predictions of the end times?

a. Earthquakes b. Pestilence c. Famine
d. All of these

8

Nature
Animals, Earth, Air

1. **E** What is the first thing to appear in the sky in Matthew?
    a. Lightning   b. The winds   c. A star   d. Clouds
2. **E** What did Jesus say was "easy and light"?
    a. His yoke   b. His Spirit   c. The river Jordan   d. Heaven
3. **E** "Give us today our daily _____."
    a. bread   b. meal   c. drink   d. light
4. **M** What did Peter find in the mouth of a fish?
    a. A ring   b. A jewel   c. A dove   d. A coin
5. **H** "Are you to be exalted to the skies?" Jesus asked _____.
    a. Tyre   b. Sidon   c. Capernaum   d. Jerusalem
6. **H** Jesus said, "You never pick _____ from thornbushes."
    a. grapes   b. figs   c. olives   d. wheat
7. **E** How many days did Jonah spend in the belly of a fish?
    a. 1   b. 2   c. 3   d. 7
8. **M** In Matthew, who first mentioned the "land of Israel"?
    a. John the Baptist   b. King Herod
    c. The wise men   d. An angel

9. **H** According to John the Baptist, where will unfruitful trees be thrown?

    a. Into fire   b. Into the sea   c. Into a pit
    d. Into the dust

10. **E** With what kind of food did Satan tempt Jesus?

    a. Honey   b. Bread   c. Fish   d. Meat

11. **H** What is the first geographic location identified in Matthew?

    a. Babylon   b. Jerusalem   c. Bethlehem
    d. The east

12. **M** Where did the five thousand sit when the disciples fed them?

    a. On the shore   b. On the grass   c. On rocks
    d. On the riverbed

13. **M** What happened on the earth when Jesus died?

    a. Earthquakes   b. Boulders split   c. Floods
    d. a and b

14. **E** To which substance did Jesus first compare the disciples?

    a. Water   b. Salt   c. Soil   d. Gold

15. **E** Which part of his body did John the Baptist lose?

    a. His foot   b. His hand   c. His head   d. His heart

16. **E** Who observed the first celestial sign in Matthew?

    a. Joseph   b. Mary   c. John the Baptist
    d. Astrologers

17. **M** What was John the Baptist's clothing made of?

    a. Sheepskin   b. Camel's hair   d. Bearskin
    d. Cotton

18. **M** According to Matthew, which of the following is Capernaum near?

    a. The sea   b. A river   c. The desert   d. The plains

19. **H** Where were the two blind men sitting at Jericho?
    a. On a mountain   b. By the road   c. In a cave
    d. On the sand
20. **H** What opened at the moment of Jesus' death?
    a. The earth   b. The sky   c. Tombs
    d. The floodgates
21. **M** Jesus told his disciples not to acquire gold, silver, and _____ on their missionary trip.
    a. diamonds   b. bronze   c. copper   d. incense
22. **H** What is the first region mentioned in Matthew?
    a. Idumea   b. Egypt   c. Judea   d. Galilee
23. **E** On what did Peter miraculously walk?
    a. A lake   b. The clouds   c. The air   d. Nothing
24. **M** What was being sold in the temple when Jesus cleared it?
    a. Jewels   b. Gold   c. Silver   d. Doves
25. **E** In the parable of the seed, the seed was eaten by what?
    a. Rats   b. Worms   c. Swine   d. Birds
26. **M** In what kind of clothing do false prophets appear?
    a. Snake's   b. Wolf's   c. Sheep's   d. Angels'
27. **M** What did Jesus walk through one Sabbath?
    a. Flowers   b. The desert   c. Grainfields   d. Water
28. **E** What type of insect did John the Baptist eat?
    a. Locusts   b. Ants   c. Bees   d. None
29. **H** Jesus told his disciples "You must be as clever as _____."
    a. owls   b. snakes   c. foxes   d. lions
30. **E** What is a solid house built upon?
    a. Wood   b. Rock   c. Water   d. Brick

31. E To what place did Jesus give Peter the key of authority?

   a. Heaven   b. Earth   c. Hell   d. The church

32. E For what did Judas betray Jesus?

   a. Gold   b. Silver   c. Bronze   d. Copper

33. E Jesus said, "My mission is to the lost _____ of the house of Israel."

   a. Jews   b. children   c. seed   d. sheep

34. M What did the Pharisees accuse the disciples of not washing?

   a. Their feet   b. Their hands   c. their cloaks   d. Their hair

35. M Where did Jesus see the first disciples?

   a. By the sea   b. On a mountain
   c. In the desert   d. In the plains

36. H Jesus said, "Don't toss your pearls before _____."

   a. dogs   b. snakes   c. goats   d. swine

37. M What did Jesus feed the four thousand?

   a. Fish   b. Fruit   c. Bread   d. a and c

38. E From which direction did the Magi come?

   a. North   b. East   c. South   d. West

39. M According to John the Baptist, what will Jesus gather into his barn?

   a. Dust   b. Swine   c. Sheep   d. Grain

40. H According to Satan, what would Jesus not strike his foot against?

   a. A stone   b. A snake   c. A pit   d. A carcass

41. H Who was the first in Matthew to mention death?

   a. The wise men   b. King Herod   c. An angel
   d. Joseph

42. **m** What is the first creature associated with Jesus?
    a. Sheep   b. A vulture   c. An ox   d. A dove
43. **m** What kind of material was the belt of John the Baptist made of?
    a. Twine   b. Rope   c. Leather   d. Wool
44. **e** Besides locusts, what did John the Baptist eat?
    a. Cactus   b. Milk   c. Bread   d. Honey
45 **e** What happened when the angel visited the Lord's tomb?
    a. The sun came out   b. The earth quaked
    c. The sky clouded up   d. It began to rain
46. **e** Symbolically, upon which natural substance was the church to be built?
    a. Clay   b. A rock   c. The clouds   d. Sand
47. **h** Jesus told his disciples that they should be as innocent as _____.
    a. cubs   b. sheep   c. hens   d. doves
48. **m** Jesus said that the _____ is the body's lamp.
    a. eye   b. heart   c. soul   d. tongue
49. **m** What is the first chapter in Matthew to record a celestial sign?
    a. 1   b. 2   c. 3   d. 5
50. **e** "The voice of one crying in the _____."
    a. night   b. wilderness   c. heavens   d. morning
51. **e** What did Jesus control on the Sea of Galilee?
    a. Lightning   b. Rain   c. Fog   d. Wind
52. **e** To which disciple did Jesus give the name of a natural substance?
    a. Thomas   b. Peter   c. Judas   d. None

53. E What kind of creature swallowed Jonah?

   a. A large fish   b. A dragon   c. A large serpent
   d. A lion

54. H What animal did Jesus use in his example of a good work done on the Sabbath?

   a. A donkey   b. A dove   c. Goats   d. Sheep

55. M Where was the first place Jesus retreated after confronting a large crowd?

   a. Peter's home   b. A cave   c. The desert
   d. A mountainside

56. M What kind of food did Satan first mention in Matthew?

   a. Meat   b. Fish   c. Bread   d. Honey

57. E On what did Jesus miraculously walk?

   a. Air   b. A lake   c. The clouds   d. A river

58. M At the transfiguration, where did the voice of God come from?

   a. The temple   b. Thunder   c. A cloud   d. A bush

59. E What was the star announcing Jesus' birth doing when it was first observed?

   a. Rising   b. Setting   c. Growing brighter
   d. Growing larger

60. E In what part of the country did John the Baptist preach?

   a. Desert   b. Mountains   c. Plains   d. Foothills

61. M Where could Peter "bind" or "loosen"?

   a. Heaven   b. Earth   c. Hell   d. a and b

62. E Jesus said, "_____ sky at night, the day will be fair."

   a. Cloudy   b. Blue   c. Red   d. Gray

63. **H** In Matthew, who first mentioned the people of Israel?
   a. Isaiah   b. Micah   c. Joseph   d. King Herod

64. **E** With what did John the Baptist baptize?
   a. Water   b. Words   c. Salt   d. Oil

65. **M** What is the first food Jesus mentions in Matthew?
   a. Fish   b. Meat   c. Honey   d. Bread

66. **H** Jesus said, "Do not give what is holy to _____."
   a. swine   b. dogs   c. snakes   d. insects

67. **E** What was Jesus' crown made of?
   a. Gold   b. Bronze   c. Flowers   d. Thorns

68. **H** In an example given by Jesus, how many sheep remained after one was lost?
   a. 11   b. 99   c. 2   d. 23

69. **H** In the parable of the pearl, where was the pearl found?
   a. In a cave   b. In a field   c. In a lake
   d. It doesn't say

70. **E** Which creature did Jesus mention in the story of Jonah?
   a. A fish   b. A lion   c. A lamb   d. A wolf

71. **H** What is the first creature mentioned in Matthew?
   a. Sheep   b. A bird   c. A camel   d. A snake

72. **H** What does not "sow or reap"?
   a. Oxen   b. Sheep   c. Birds   d. Cows

73. **M** According to Jesus, who will "inherit the land"?
   a. The lowly   b. The sorrowing
   c. The single-hearted   d. The persecuted

74. **M** In one parable, what kind of treasure was buried in a field?
   a. Pearls   b. Gold   c. Silver   d. It doesn't say

75. **E** From what did John the Baptist say God could raise Abraham's children?

   a. Mountains   b. Trees   c. Stones   d. Rivers

76. **E** Which heavenly sign was associated with Jesus' birth?

   a. A blinding light   b. Clouds   c. Lightning
   d. A star

77. **H** In Matthew, what term is used to describe the wise men's country?

   a. The desert   b. The east   c. The west
   d. The hinterlands

78. **E** When Jesus and Peter climbed into the boat, what calmed down?

   a. The wind   b. The rain   c. The hail   d. The fish

79. **E** What happened in the sky at Jesus' death?

   a. Lightning   b. A star   c. Rain   d. Darkness

80. **M** From where did Jesus get his temple tax?

   a. A widow   b. A fish   c. A dove   d. A field

81. **M** On what did the disciples lay their cloaks for Jesus?

   a. A camel   b. The road
   c. The foal of a donkey   d. The water

9

The Passion

1. **M** Where were the chief priests assembled when they plotted to arrest Jesus?
   a. A lake   b. A courtyard   c. A synagogue
   d. A palace
2. **E** What was poured on Jesus' head at the house of Simon the leper?
   a. Water   b. Perfume   c. Wine   d. Oil
3. **M** What time of day did Jesus and the disciples share the Last Supper?
   a. Noon   b. Late afternoon   c. Early evening
   d. Late evening
4. **H** By which title did Jesus refer to himself just before the Last Supper?
   a. Teacher   b. Messiah   c. Son of David
   d. Son of man
5. **E** What did Jesus do first at Gethsemane?
   a. He cried   b. He prayed   c. He taught
   d. He slept
6. **M** After Jesus found the disciples asleep at Gethsemane for the last time, what did he tell them to do?
   a. Wake up   b. Keep sleeping   c. Pray   d. Nothing
7. **H** What weapons were used at Jesus' arrest?
   a. Swords and clubs   b. Sticks and stones
   c. Swords and chains   d. None

8. **E** According to Caiaphas, what had Jesus done to deserve death?

   a. Embezzlement   b. Blasphemy   c. Treason
   d. Nothing

9. **H** With what words did Judas betray Jesus?

   a. "My dear teacher"   b. "Master!"
   d. "My Lord and my God"   d. "Peace, Rabbi"

10. **M** To whom did Peter deny knowing Jesus?

    a. John   b. A guard   c. The centurion
    d. A servant girl

11. **E** To whom was Jesus led after the interrogation before Caiaphas?

    a. Pontius Pilate   b. Herod Antipas   c. Caesar
    d. Herod the Great

12. **M** Who warned Pilate about Jesus?

    a. Nicodemus   b. Pilate's wife   c. Peter
    d. An angel

13. **E** Pilate claimed to be innocent of Jesus' _____.

    a. spirit   b. body   c. blood   d. family

14. **M** Who rolled the stone across the entrance to Jesus' tomb?

    a. An angel   b. Joseph of Arimathea   c. God
    d. It doesn't say

15. **H** Who was guarding Jesus while he was on the cross?

    a. Peter and John   b. Nicodemus
    c. The centurion   d. Martha

16. **E** At the crucifixion, for whom did the crowd think Jesus called?

    a. David   b. Moses   c. Enoch   d Elijah

17. **H** What was the color of the robe the soldiers put on Jesus?

    a. Blue   b. Brown   c. Scarlet   d. It doesn't say

18. **E** Who carried Jesus' cross?
    a. Simon the Cyrene   b. Peter   c. The centurion
    d. The soldiers
19. **E** How much wine did Jesus have while on the cross?
    a. One taste   b. Several drinks   c. A bottle
    d. None
20. **M** How did Jesus refer to himself at his trial?
    a. Messiah   b. Son of man   c. Christ
    d. Son of God
21. **M** What did Jesus call Judas at his arrest?
    a. Satan   b. Hypocrite   c. Traitor   d. Friend
22. **H** Which Old Testament prophet spoke of Judas, the money, and the field?
    a. Ezekiel   b. Jeremiah   c. Isaiah   d. Obadiah
23. **M** Who convinced the crowds to pick Barabbas over Jesus?
    a. The chief priests   b. The elders
    c. The scribes   d. a and b
24. **E** How did Jesus feel as he prayed at Gethsemane?
    a. Confused   b. Joyful   c. Sorrowful   d. Peaceful
25. **E** What symbolized the New Covenant at the Last Supper?
    a. Bread   b. Wine   c. Dates   d. A lamb
26. **H** How did Judas address Jesus at the Last Supper?
    a. King   b. The Christ   c. Messiah   d. Rabbi
27. **M** How did the chief priests arrest Jesus?
    a. By kidnapping him   b. By exposing him
    c. By tricking him   d. By bribing him
28. **E** What did Judas receive for betraying Jesus?
    a. Bronze   b. Gold   c. Silver   d. Copper

29. **H** On which feast day did the disciples prepare for the Last Supper?

    a. Jubilee   b. The first of Nisan   c. Atonement
    d. Unleavened Bread

30. **M** Where does Matthew say that Judas Iscariot died?

    a. The Blood Field   b. Potter's Field
    c. Golgotha   d. He doesn't

31. **E** What did the chief priests call the betrayal money?

    a. Traitor's money   b. Black money
    c. Blood money   d. Evil money

32. **M** How did onlookers recognize that Peter was Jesus' disciple?

    a. By his manner   b. By his accent
    c. By his clothes   d. By his hair

33. **H** What did Caiaphas do to his robes at the trial?

    a. He tightened them   b. he changed them
    c. He removed them   d. He tore them

34. **E** Who took the stand at Jesus' trial?

    a. Martha   b. A Roman soldier
    c. False witnesses   d. John

35. **M** Who, according to Matthew's Gospel, cut off the ear of the high priest's servant?

    a. John   b. Judas   c. Peter   d. It doesn't say

36. **H** How many women were present at the crucifixion?

    a. 1   b. 2   c. 3   d. It doesn't say

37. **E** What did Jesus do immediately before he died?

    a. He whispered   b. He prayed   c. He cried out
    d. He drank wine

38. **E** What did the soldiers use to strike Jesus on the head?

    a. A club   b. A reed   c. A sword   d. A rock

39. **H** Besides blaming themselves, whom did the crowds make responsible for Jesus' crucifixion?
a. Their children   b. Their forefathers   c. Pilate
d. Judas

40. **M** At what time of the day during the crucifixion did darkness start to cover the land?
a. 9 a.m.   b. Noon   c. 3 p.m.   d. 6 p.m.

41. **E** Before the crucifixion, what meal was prepared for Jesus?
a. The Sabbath   b. Passover   c. Jubilee
d. Bar Mitzvah

42. **E** Who went to the chief priests to betray Jesus?
a. Peter   b. Thomas   c. Judas   d. John

43. **E** What did Jesus refer to as "the fruit of the vine"?
a. Apples   b. His body   c. His blood   d. Figs

44. **M** What were the disciples doing in Gethsemane when Jesus returned from praying?
a. Talking   b. Hiding   c. Praying   d. Sleeping

45. **H** In Matthew, how did Judas betray Jesus?
a. With a kiss   b. With a word   c. With a smile
d. With a sword

46. **M** When did Jesus predict his betrayal?
a. Before the meal   b. During the meal
c. After the meal   d. He didn't

47. **H** What is the name of the field purchased with Judas's money?
a. Blood Field   b. Potter's Field   c. Traitor's Field
d. Field of Death

48. **H** How did Peter react when he was identified as Jesus' disciple?

    a. He kept silent   b. He yelled   c. He cried   d. He swore

49. **M** On what grounds did the chief priests suggest the release of Barabbas in place of Jesus?

    a. Rivalry   b. Jealousy   c. Vindictiveness   d. Greed

50. **H** At the trial of Jesus, whom did Peter sit next to?

    a. Priests   b. Guards   c. Scribes   d. John

51. **E** What happened to the disciples after the betrayal of Jesus?

    a. They hid   b. They deserted him
    c. They fell asleep   d. They prayed

52. **E** What quality of wine was offered to Jesus on the cross?

    a. Cheap   b. Average   c. Good   d. It wasn't offered

53. **E** What happened to Jesus prior to the crucifixion?

    a. He became sick   b. His legs were broken
    c. He was stabbed   d. He was scourged

54. **H** Where was Jesus crowned with thorns?

    a. Pilate's residence   b. Golgotha
    c. The praetorium   d. The courtyard

55. **M** What was placed in Jesus' right hand before the crucifixion?

    a. A cup   b. A reed   c. A crown   d. A nail

56. **E** Who wrapped Jesus' body in fresh linen?

    a. His mother   b. Nicodemus
    c. Joseph of Arimathea   d. Martha

57. **E** After Jesus died, what suddenly broke open?

    a. The clouds   b. Tombs   c. Flowers   d. Mouths

58. **M** What was the potter's field used for?
    a. To build a home   b. To erect the cross
    c. To plant wheat   d. As a cemetery
59. **H** How many times did Jesus speak to Pontius Pilate?
    a. Once   b. Twice   c. 3 times   d. Not once
60. **M** Where was Peter when he first denied being Jesus' follower?
    a. In the courtyard   b. In Pilate's home
    c. In the streets   d. At Golgotha
61. **H** Whose house was the scene of the Last Supper?
    a. Peter's   b. John's   c. Matthew's   d. It doesn't say
62. **E** Why did the chief priests not want to arrest Jesus during a feast?
    a. Fear of God   b. Fear of riots
    c. It wasn't allowed   d. It wouldn't be noticed
63. **E** For how many pieces of silver did Judas betray Jesus?
    a. 6   b. 12   c. 30   d. 60
64. **E** To whom did Jesus refer when he said, "It would have been better not to have been born?
    a. Thomas   b. Judas   c. Pilate   d. Caesar
65. **H** How many times did Jesus pray in Gethsemane?
    a. Once   b. Twice   c. 3 times   d. 4 times
66. **M** How many disciples did Jesus take to pray with him in Gethsemane?
    a. 1   b. 2   c. 3   d. All of them
67. **H** Where did the disciples go immediately after the Last Supper?
    a. The Mount of Olives   b. The River Jordan
    c. Peter's house   d. Capernaum

68. E What did Jesus bless at the Last Supper?
   a. Bread   b. Olives   c. Dates   d. Doves
69. M What does "Golgotha" mean?
   a. Calvary   b. Place of Blood
   c. Place of the Skull   d. Potter's Field
70. E How did Judas Iscariot die?
   a. He stabbed himself   b. He hanged himself
   c. He poisoned himself   d. He starved himself
71. M How did Caiaphas address Jesus at his trial?
   a. Savior   b. King   c. Christ   d. Messiah
72. H At the betrayal, how many angels could Jesus have called upon?
   a. 6 legions   b. 12 legions   c. 24 legions
   d. Innumerable
73. E After Peter denied Jesus three times, what did he do?
   a. He hid   b. He prayed   c. He cried
   d. He killed himself
74. H Where was Peter when he denied Jesus the third time?
   a. At the gate   b. By the door   c. At home
   d. It doesn't say
75. E What was Jesus' tomb made of?
   a. Rock   b. Brick   c. Wood   d. It doesn't say
76. M What was Jesus dressed in after the soldiers finished mocking him?
   a. The same clothes   b. A shroud   c. Nothing
   d. His own clothes
77. M What time of day did Jesus die?
   a. Early morning   b. Noon   c. Mid-afternoon
   d. Late afternoon

78. E Whom did the people look for to save Jesus from the cross?

   a. Elijah   b. Enoch   c. An angel   d. God

79. M Where was Peter when he denied Jesus the second time?

   a. By the fire   b. At the gate
   c. In the courtyard   d. It doesn't say

80. E Who was to decide whether Jesus or Barabbas should be freed?

   a. Herod Antipas   b. Pilate   c. Jesus   d. The crowd

81. M How many days before his arrest did Jesus forewarn his disciples?

   a. 1 day   b. 2 days   c. 3 days   d. 1 week

82. H Where was the home of Simon the leper?

   a. Bethany   b. Bethsaida   c. Cana   d. Capernaum

83. E At the Last Supper, which did Jesus take first— bread or wine?

   a. Bread   b. Wine   c. Both together
   d. It doesn't say

84. M At the Last Supper, what title did Jesus give himself?

   a. Messiah   b. Son of Man   c. Son of God   d. King

85. H How many of the disciples claimed that they would never deny Jesus?

   a. 1   b. 3   c. None of them   d. All of them

86. M Were did Jesus appear first after his resurrection?

   a. Rome   b. The Decapolis   c. Galilee   d. Samaria

87. E What sign immediately appeared after Jesus' death, causing the centurion to believe?

   a. An earthquake   b. A flood   c. Lightning
   d. Thunder

88. E With which title did the soldiers mock Jesus?
   a. King of the Jews   b. Lamb of God
   c. Son of God   d. The Christ

89. M Why did Pilate give in to the crowd's wish for crucifixion?
   a. He was bribed
   b. He thought the crowd would riot
   c. He saw that he wasn't accomplishing anything
   d. b and c

90. M What was mixed with the wine given to Jesus on the cross?
   a. Gall   b. Myrrh   c. Oil   d. Herbs

91. H Who was the last person to leave the scene of Jesus' burial besides "the other Mary"?
   a. Mary Magdalene   b. Martha   c. Peter   d. John

92. E After Jesus died, what was torn in two?
   a. The sky   b. A cloak   c. A curtain   d. A cross

93. H Whose bodies were raised from the dead immediately after Jesus died?
   a. Those of the saints'
   b. Those of Jesus' relatives'
   c. Those of Abraham and Moses
   d. Those of Lazarus and John the Baptist

94. E In his prayer at Gethsemane, what did Jesus ask to be taken from him?
   a. Bread   b. A cup   c. A Sword   d. Death

95. H What did Jesus and the disciples do immediately after the Last Supper?
   a. They slept   b. They prayed   c. They sang
   d. They argued

96. M Who paid Judas Iscariot for his betrayal of Jesus?
   a. A chief priest   b. Pilate   c. Herod Antipas
   d. A Roman soldier

10

From Heaven Above
God, Prayer, the Risen Christ

1. **E** What parable compares God's kingdom to a buried treasure?
   a. The treasure b. The mustard seed
   c. The weeds d. The net
2. **M** How many times did God appear to Joseph?
   a. Once b. 3 times c. 4 times d. Not once
3. **E** In Matthew, to whom did God first speak?
   a. Mary b. Jesus c. Joseph d. Simeon
4. **E** From where did God's voice first come in Matthew?
   a. The heavens b. A bush c. A fire d. The clouds
5. **H** In Matthew, how many times does Satan speak of Jesus as the "Son of God"?
   a. Once b. Twice c. 3 times d. Not once
6. **H** How many Beatitudes directly mention heaven?
   a. 3 b. 4 c. 5 d. None
7. **H** He who swears by heaven is swearing by God's _____.
   a. Footstool b. Son c. Throne d. Word
8. **E** Jesus said we will receive what we pray for, provided we have _____.
   a. forgiven b. authority c. good intentions d. faith

9. **E** What symbol did Jesus use in talking about riches and heaven?

    a. A staff   b. A stone   c. A needle   d. A house

10. **E** How many lines in the Lord's Prayer mention heaven?

    a. 1   b. 2   c. 3   d. 4

11. **M** If we keep our deeds of mercy secret, what will the Father do?

    a. Repay us   b. Condemn us   c. Enlighten us
    d. Forgive us

12. **H** Through which prophet in Matthew did God speak first?

    a. Isaiah   b. Jeremiah   c. Daniel   d. Moses

13. **E** Jesus said, "Ask, and you shall _____."

    a. be asked   b. receive   c. overcome   d. find

14. **M** Upon what will the apostles sit while judging the twelve tribes?

    a. The Mount of Olives   b. Footstools
    c. Thrones   d. The altar

15. **H** The women clasped the risen Christ's _____ and worshiped him.

    a. arm   b. robes   c. hands   d. feet

16. **M** At the second coming of Jesus, what will be shaken?

    a. God's wrath   b. Heavenly bodies
    c. The clouds   d. The sun

17. **H** Jesus said, "In your prayers, do not _____."

    a. Act proudly   b. Become disturbed
    c. Rattle on   d. Become selfish

18. **M** Who will be least in God's kingdom?

    a. Perpetual sinners   b. Those who are rich
    c. Those who are unbaptized
    d. Those who break the commandments

19. **M** At which event did God speak to the people in his own voice?

    a. Jesus' baptism   b. The temptation
    c. Joseph's dream   d. The feast at Cana

20. **E** Whom did Jesus entrust with the keys of the kingdom of heaven?

    a. John   b. Peter   c. All twelve disciples   d. No one

21. **H** What appears to be God's first demand of Jesus?

    a. Obedience to parents   b. Prayer
    c. His temptation   d. His baptism

22. **M** What did Jesus call those who pray in public for attention?

    a. Wolves   b. Hypocrites   c. False prophets
    d. Pagans

23. **E** Who will find it most difficult to pass through the eye of a needle than to enter the Kingdom of heaven?

    a. The rich   b. The adulterous   c. Blasphemers
    d. The proud

24. **E** Jesus said, "The one who seeks, _____."

    a. finds   b. overcomes   c. understands
    d. is healed

25. **E** The Son of man will return accompanied by _____.

    a. the apostles   b. his mother   c. angels   d. Elijah

26. **M** What will the Father grant to those who pray in Jesus' name?

    a. Peace   b. Humility   c. The kingdom
    d. "Anything"

27. **H** How many angels could Jesus summon at any moment?

    a. 6 legions   b. 12 legions   c. A myriad
    d. Innumerable legions

28. **H** Jesus compared scribes who became his disciples to _____.

   a. yeast   b. army captains   c. owners of houses
   d. prodigal sons

29. **M** In what chapter in Matthew is God first mentioned?
   a. 1   b. 2   c. 3   d. 5

30. **M** How did Jesus refer to God when confronting Satan?
   a. Father in heaven   b. Redeemer
   c. The Creator   d. The Lord your God

31. **M** "Soon you will see the Son of Man seated at the right hand of _____."
   a. the Father   b. Power   c. the Judge   d. the hosts

32. **E** To whom will the Father give good things if they ask him?
   a. The holy ones   b. The repentant
   c. The righteous   d. Anyone

33. **E** John said, "Repent, for the _____ is at hand."
   a. Baptist   b. God   c. the Savior
   d. Kingdom of heaven

34. **E** What kind of treasure should we store up?
   a. Earthly   b. Prayerful   c. Heavenly   d. None

35. **M** Not a single _____ falls to the ground without the Father's consent.
   a. lamb   b. soul   c. sheep   d. sparrow

36. **E** According to Jesus, what must be fulfilled before heaven and earth "passes away"?
   a. Redemption   b. Righteousness   c. The Law
   d. Lives

37. **M** In Matthew, what accompanied the angel's appearance after the resurrection?
   a. A flock of doves   b. An earthquake
   c. Lightning   d. Nothing

38. E Jesus said, "Let no man separate what _____ has joined."
   a. God   b. the Son   c. the Spirit   d. heaven
39. E How many times did God speak to King Herod?
   a. Once   b. Twice   c. 3 times   d. Not once
40. M To whom has God revealed that which he has hidden from the learned?
   a. The meek   b. The poor   c. Children
   d. The orphaned
41. M Whose holiness must be surpassed in order to gain entrance to God's kingdom?
   a. The scribes   b. The Pharisees
   c. The Sadducees   d. a and b
42. E In Matthew, which name means "God is with us"?
   a. Immanuel   b. David   c. Jesse   d. Jesus
43. E "Give to Caesar what is Caesar's, but give to _____ what is God's."
   a. me   b. prayer   c. God   d. no one
44. E The risen Christ said, "Full authority has been given to me both in _____ and _____."
   a. heaven, earth   b. truth, love   c. Judah, Israel
   d. judgment, salvation
45. E In Matthew, what name is indicative of God's presence?
   a. Immanuel   b. David   c. Jesus   d. Gabriel
46. H What did God "clothe in splendor"?
   a. The mountains   b. Flowers   c. The fields
   d. The animals
47. E "Unless you change and become like _____, you cannot enter God's kingdom."
   a. John the Baptist   b. children   c. me
   d. the prophets

48. **H** What does Jesus' prayer, "Eloi, Eloi, lama sabachthani," refer to?

   a. Being forsaken   b. Giving up the spirit
   c. Forgiveness   d. Repentance

49. **M** Jesus said, "There is only _____ who is good."

   a. the Father   b. the Spirit   c. One   d. the Son

50. **H** From where will people come to share with the patriarchs the banquet in heaven?

   a. North and south   b. East and west
   c. Jerusalem   d. Rome

51. **M** Regarding _____ Jesus said, "With God all things are possible"?

   a. Salvation   b. Healing   c. Purity   d. Forgiveness

52. **M** In Matthew, who first addressed Jesus as "Son of God"?

   a. Joseph   b. Peter   c. Satan   d. John the Baptist

53. **E** Who said, "God can raise up children to Abraham from these very stones"?

   a. Jesus   b. John the Baptist   c. Peter   d. James

54. **M** Jesus said, "You cannot give yourself to God and _____."

   a. Satan   b. lust   c. self   d. money

55. **E** What adjective describes the gate that leads to heaven?

   a. Narrow   b. Wide   c. Immeasurable   d. Eternal

56. **M** Which parable compares God's kingdom to a king?

   a. The net   b. The tenants   c. The treasure
   d. The wedding banquet

57. **H** How did God first speak to Joseph?

   a. Through Jesus   b. In a vision
   c. Through an angel   d. In a prophecy

58. **M** Through which prophet did God say, "Out of Egypt I have called my son"?
   a. Hosea   b. Micah   c. Zechariah   d. Malachi
59. **E** In Matthew, who first preached the Kingdom of God?
   a. Mary   b. Jesus   c. John the Baptist   d. Joseph
60. **H** How many Beatitudes promise a vision of God?
   a. 1   b. 2   c. 4   d. All of them
61. **E** Who declared that he could destroy and rebuild the temple in three days?
   a. The high priest   b. Judas   c. Pontius Pilate
   d. Jesus
62. **E** On what will the Son of man someday come from heaven?
   a. Clouds   b. Angels' wings   c. Lightning
   d. Thunder
63. **H** According to John the Baptist, what could God raise up from stones?
   a. Prophets   b. Water   c. Abraham's children
   d. Mountains
64. **H** Who was the second prophet that God spoke through in Matthew?
   a. Zechariah   b. Micah   c. Isaiah   d. Ezekiel
65. **M** How many times did God appear to Mary?
   a. Once   b. Twice   c. 5 times   d. Not once
66. **E** After Christ's resurrection, who said, "Do not be afraid"?
   a. Jesus   b. An angel   c. A Roman guard
   d. The Father

67. H Jesus said, "When you pray, do not keep on babbling like _____."
    a. pagans   b. the Romans   c. the Sadducees   d. the Zealots

68. E Who will not forgive us if we do not forgive others?
    a. The Son   b. The Father   c. The angels   d. Our friends

69. M By what name is God first addressed in Matthew?
    a. God   b. Father   c. Lord   d. Yahweh

70. E According to Jesus, where should one pray?
    a. Everywhere   b. The temple   c. Anywhere   d. In one's room

71. E In Matthew, who first heard God's voice?
    a. John the Baptist   b. Peter   c. Joseph   d. James

72. M In Jesus' prayer on the cross, what does "Eloi" refer to?
    a. The Spirit   b. Heaven   c. God   d. Elijah

73. H Which parable compares God's kingdom to good seed?
    a. The leaven   b. The weeds   c. The pearl   d. The two sons

74. E Whoever does God's will is what to Jesus?
    a. Brother   b. Sister   c. Mother   d. All of these

75. M What two masters do some people worship?
    a. God and money   b. God and Satan   c. God and lust   d. God and gods

76. E Whose house should be called a house of prayer?
    a. God's   b. Peter's   c. Christians'   d. The Sadducees'

77. E "Sell your possessions, and then you will have _____ in heaven."
    a. fulfillment   b. eternal life   c. favor   d. treasure

78. **M** What is the correct title for the angel who visited Joseph?
    a. Angel of light   b. Angel of the Lord
    c. The beloved angel   d. Guardian angel
79. **M** In Matthew, what was the angel's name?
    a. Gabriel   b. Raphael   c. Michael
    d. It doesn't say
80. **M** To whom did Jesus talk about personal riches and entry to heaven?
    a. The Samaritan   b. The disciples
    c. Nicodemus   d. Joseph of Arimathea
81. **E** Who in heaven constantly beholds the Father's face?
    a. The dead   b. The patriarchs   c. Angels
    d. No one
82. **H** Which parable uses a lake to symbolize an aspect of God's kingdom?
    a. The leaven   b. The weeds   c. The pearl
    d. The net
83. **H** Jesus said, "Do not call anyone on earth your _____."
    a. savior   b. God   c. prophet   d. father
84. **E** Which parable compares God's kingdom to yeast?
    a. The leaven   b. The weeds   c. The pearl
    d. The mustard seed
85. **M** How did Jesus reveal the mysteries of the Kingdom of heaven?
    a. Parables   b. Prophecies   c. Good deeds
    d. He didn't
86. **M** Jesus said, "Where _____ or _____ are gathered in my name, there I am."
    a. 1 or 2   b. 2 or 3   c. one or more   d. many or few

87. E How should we fast in a godly way?
    a. Openly   b. Secretly   c. In great length
    d. With much prayer
88. E Who will escort Jesus at his second coming?
    a. All the dead   b. The saints   c. God   d. Angels
89. M What does Jesus' greatest commandment deal with?
    a. Love for God   b. Heaven   c. Love for neighbor
    d. Prayer
90. H Who received from Jesus the knowledge of the mysteries of the Kingdom of heaven?
    a. The disciples   b. Mary Magdalene
    c. The meek   d. John the Baptist
91. E What must we seek first in order to receive life's necessities?
    a. Friendship   b. Forgiveness   c. Purity
    d. The kingdom
92. H Who shuts the doors of God's kingdom in men's faces?
    a. The scribes   b. The Pharisees   c. The priests
    d. a and b
93. E Why should we not swear by heaven?
    a. Heaven is pure   b. It is God's throne
    c. It is blasphemy   d. None of these

General Questions
History and Archaeology

1. What does the word *gospel* mean?
   a. salvation   b. good tidings   c. truth
   d. immortality
2. Which are the synoptic Gospels?
   a. Matthew, Luke   b. Matthew, Mark, Luke
   c. Luke, Matthew   d. Matthew, Mark, John
3. Which title did Pontius Pilate hold?
   a. prefect   b. procurator   c. governor   d. king
4. Who wrote the Book of Acts?
   a. Mark   b. Luke   c. John   d. Paul
5. Which fortress in Jerusalem did King Herod build?
   a. the Citadel   b. Herodius   c. Antonia   d. Masada
6. What does the disciple Peter's name mean?
   a. foundation   b. rock   c. the faithful one
   d. man of God
7. In which language were the Gospels written?
   a. Latin   b. Hebrew   c. Greek   d. Syriac
8. Which Gospel writer was a tax collector?
   a. John   b. Luke   c. Matthew   d. Mark
9. What does Gabriel's name mean?
   a. God-light   b. true God   c. man of God   d. messenger

10. Who were the Jewish fanatics in Jesus' day?
    a. Pharisees   b. Sadducees   c. Zealots   d. scribes
11. What does John mean by *Logos*?
    a. intervention   b. savior   c. mystery   d. divine word
12. Who were the religious conservatives of Jesus' day?
    a. Pharisees   b. Sadducees   c. Zealots   d. Essenes
13. What was the common language of Palestine in Jesus' time?
    a. Hebrew   b. Aramaic   c. Greek   d. Latin
14. When did Titus attack and destroy Jerusalem?
    a. AD 29   b. AD 34   c. AD 70   d. AD 110
15. Who built Caesarea?
    a. Herod Antipas   b. King Herod
    c. Titus   d. Pontius Pilate
16. Whose dethronement led to the census recorded in Luke's Gospel?
    a. Archelaus   b. Philip   c. Herod   d. Theophilus
17. What was the Praetorium?
    a. the Sanhedrin   b. a Roman prison
    c. Herod's palace   d. Caiphas's home
18. What does Mary's name mean?
    a. God-bearer   b. light   c. stubbornness
    d. blessed
19. Which was the elite Jewish sect during Jesus' day?
    a. Essenes   b. Pharisees   c. Sadducees   d. Zealots
20. Which kind of Greek were the Gospels written in?
    a. Koine   b. Ionic   c. Doric   d. Aeolian
21. Which language did Jesus use?
    a. Greek   b. Hebrew   c. Aramaic   d. Syriac
22. What does Matthew's name mean?
    a. heavenly one   b. light-bearer
    c. gift of God   d. free spirit

23. What is the Greek word for *gospel*?
    a. gospel   b. kerygma   c. evangelion   d. Hellenist
24. Who were the publicans during Jesus' time?
    a. legal advisers   b. scribes   c. tax collectors   d. priests
25. Who was ruling in Judea when Jesus was a child?
    a. Archelaus   b. Pontius Pilate   c. Herod Antipas   d. Philip
26. Whose fortress was built near Bethlehem?
    a. Pontius Pilate   b. Herod   c. Tiberius Caesar   d. Nero
27. Which kind of money is mentioned most often in the Gospels?
    a. pound   b. talent   c. denarius   d. shekel
28. During Jesus' day, who ruled in Jerusalem?
    a. Herod Antipas   b. Pontius Pilate   c. Philip
    d. King Herod
29. Which was the capital city of Herod Antipas?
    a. Japha   b. Capernaum   c. Tiberias   d. Sepphoris
30. Who was emperor of Rome at the time of Jesus' birth?
    a. Tiberius   b. Julius   c. Titus   d. Augustus
31. Who was the oldest son of King Herod the Great?
    a. Archelaus   b. Philip   c. Herod Antipas   d. Coponius
32. Which of King Herod's sons ruled in Palestine as ethnarch of Judea?
    a. Pontius Pilate   b. Herod Antipas   c. Philip   d. Archelaus
33. Who was ruling in Galilee when Jesus died?
    a. King Herod   b. Herod Antipas   c. Titus
    d. Pontius Pilate

Geography

1. Which of the following was closest to Jerusalem?
   a. Jericho   b. Bethlehem   c. Arimathea
   d. Nazareth
2. Which direction was Galilee in relation to Jerusalem?
   a. north   b. south   c. east   d. west
3. What other name does John give to the Sea of Galilee?
   a. Great Sea   b. Huleh   c. Lake Tiberias   d. Salt Sea
4. What does the name of the city Magdala mean?
   a. fortress   b. tower   c. crossroad   d. temple
5. What does Gethsemane mean?
   a. land of sorrows   b. caravan   c. oil press
   d. orchard
6. In which city was King Herod's amphitheater located?
   a. Jericho   b. Tiberias   c. Capernaum   d. Cana
7. Who baptized people at Bethany?
   a. Jesus   b. John the Baptist   c. Peter   d. James
8. Which village was on the Mount of Olives?
   a. Bethany   b. Shiloh   c. Bethlehem   d. Bethphage
9. Where was Samaria in relation to Jerusalem?
   a. north   b. south   c. east   d. west
10. From which town in Palestine did Nathanael come?
    a. Nazareth   b. Capernaum   c. Jericho   d. Cana
11. What does *Decapolis* mean?
    a. Ten Virtues   b. Ten Kingdoms   c. Ten Commandments
    d. Ten Cities
12. Which of the following was closest to the Sea of Galilee?
    a. Capernaum   b. Cana   c. Nazareth   D. Jericho

13. From which of the following is "Palestine" derived?
    a. Canaan   b. Israel   c. Philistine   d. Zion
14. Where did most of Jesus' ministry occur?
    a. Jerusalem   b. Judea   c. Galilee   d. Jordan River
15. Where was the Place of the Skull?
    a. Gethsemane   b. the Praetorium   c. Bethlehem
    d. Golgotha
16. How many palaces did King Herod have in Jerusalem?
    a. 1   b. 2   c. 4   d. none
17. On which part of the Fertile Crescent does Palestine lay?
    a. northeast   b. southwest   c. central   d. southeast
18. In which valley is the Garden of Gethsemane?
    a. Rift   b. Jezreel   c. Megiddo   d. Kidron
19. In Jesus' time, what was the Mediterranean Sea known as?
    a. Salt Sea   b. Great Sea   c. Philistine Sea
    d. Sea of Canaan
20. What was the significance of Megiddo for the people of Jesus' day?
    a. battleground   b. river source   c. temple site
    d. mineral deposit
21. Where do most of the events in the synoptic Gospels occur?
    a. Jerusalem   b. Galilee   c. Jordan River   d. the desert
22. What does the name Bethlehem mean?
    a. house of prayer   b. city of light   c. house of bread
    d. little town
23. In which city did Jesus carry out much of his ministry?
    a. Nazareth   b. Capernaum   c. Tiberias   d. Sepphoris
24. Which city does Matthew refer to as Jesus' own?
    a. Bethlehem   b. Nazareth   c. Jerusalem   d. Capernaum

25. Upon how many hills is Jerusalem built?
    a. 1   b. 2   c. 3   d. none
26. Where did Jesus change water into wine?
    a. Capernaum   b. Cana   c. Nazareth   d. Jerusalem
27. In which city did Jesus first teach in a synagogue?
    a. Jerusalem   b. Nazareth   c. Cana   d. Capernaum
28. What was Jerusalem's original name?
    a. Jerusalem   b. Salem   c. Jeru   d. Canaan
29. In which city does John say that Jesus performed his first miracle?
    a. Bethlehem   b. Jericho   c. Nazareth   d. Cana
30. Where do Matthew and Luke say that Jesus began his public ministry?
    a. Jerusalem   b. Nazareth   c. Capernaum   d. Jericho
31. What name does Matthew give to the Sea of Galilee?
    a. Sea of Galilee   b. Chinereth   c. Gennesareth   d. Huleh
32. Which Galilean town did Jesus curse for its unbelief?
    a. Tiberias   b. Nazareth   c. Capernaum   d. Sepphoris
33. Which mountain divides the coastal plain of Palestine in two?
    a. Mount Hebron   b. Mount Hermon   c. Mount Nebo   d. Mount Carmel

Unique Features

1. Which Gospel is distinct from the other three?
   a. John   b. Mark   c. Luke   d. Matthew
2. Which Gospel does not mention the death of John the Baptist?
   a. Matthew   b. Mark   c. Luke   d. John

3. Which Gospel was written by a physician?
   a. Matthew   b. Luke   c. John   d. Mark
4. Which Gospel describes how Jesus washed the disciples' feet?
   a. John   b. Mark   c. Luke   d. Matthew
5. Which idea is emphasized in John's Gospel?
   a. belief   b. the Messiah   c. prophecy
   d. fatherhood of God
6. Which Gospel pays particular attention to women?
   a. Mark   b. Luke   c. John   d. Matthew
7. Which Gospel is the first half of a two-part work?
   a. Matthew   b. Mark   c. Luke   d. John
8. How many disciples were called by Jesus at the Sea of Galilee?
   a. 1   b. 2   c. 3   d. 4
9. Which Gospel identifies Capernaum as Jesus' home?
   a. Matthew   b. Mark   c. Luke   d. John
10. Which Gospel speaks the most about judgment?
    a. Matthew   b. Mark   c. Luke   d. John
11. Which Gospel writer mentions the Magi?
    a. Matthew   b. Luke   c. Mark   d. John
12. Which Gospel is the shortest?
    a. Matthew   b. Mark   c. Luke   d. John
13. Which Gospel talks the most about fulfillment of Old Testament prophecy?
    a. Luke   b. John   c. Matthew   d. Mark
14. Which Gospel writer refers to his book as a *gospel*?
    a. Matthew   b. Mark and John   c. John   d. none
15. Which Gospel was addressed primarily to Jews?
    a. Matthew   b. John   c. Luke   d. Mark
16. Which Gospel writer was an "eye-witness"?
    a. Luke   b. John   c. Mark   d. Matthew

17. Which Gospel records the most miracles?
    a. John   b. Matthew   c. Mark   d. Luke
18. What is the most characteristic form of Jesus' teaching in the Gospels?
    a. parables   b. sayings   c. prayer   d. metaphors
19. What is the theme of Matthew's Gospel?
    a. friendship   b. conversion   c. love   d. kingship
20. Which Gospel does not mention the Lord's Supper?
    a. Luke   b. John   c. Matthew   d. Mark
21. What is the theme of John's Gospel?
    a. companionship   b. prayer   c. sorrow
    d. Christ's deity
22. In which Gospel does the dove descend on Jesus in bodily form?
    a. Matthew   b. Mark   c. Luke   d. John
23. Which Gospel stresses numbers?
    a. Matthew   b. John   c. Luke   d. Mark
24. Which Gospel mentions Jesus' confrontation with Herod Antipas?
    a. Matthew   b. Luke   c. John   d. Mark
25. Which Gospel mentions the miracle at Cana?
    a. John   b. Mark   c. Matthew   d. Luke
26. Which Gospel has the parable of the prodigal son?
    a. John   b. Luke   c. Matthew   d. Mark
27. Which Gospel does not list the twelve disciples as a group?
    a. Matthew   b. Mark   c. Luke   d. John
28. What is the theme of Luke's Gospel?
    a. Jesus and sinners   b. the Word   c. the Spirit
    d. holiness

29. Which idea is predominant in Mark?
    a. love   b. help   c. the Word   d. belief
30. Which Gospel contains the fewest parables?
    a. Matthew   b. Mark   c. Luke   d. John
31. Which Gospel writer is the one whom Jesus loved?
    a. Mark   b. John   c. Luke   d. Matthew
32. Which Gospel portrays Christ as a miracle worker?
    a. John   b. Mark   c. Luke   d. Matthew
33. Which Gospel stresses Christ as the "Word"?
    a. Mark   b. Luke   c. John   d. Matthew
34. Which Gospel admits that not all of Jesus' sayings and deeds have been recorded?
    a. Matthew   b. Mark   c. Luke   d. John

Answers

Chapter 1

1. d Matt. 1:16
2. d 1:25
3. b 1:8
4. b 2:15
5. c 1:20
6. a 2:16
7. a 2:1–2
8. c 3:1
9. c 1:19
10. b 1:23
11. b 1:4
12. c 2:11
13. d 2:13
14. d 2:2
15. b 1:14
16. b 1:18
17. b 2:15
18. c 2:23
19. a 1:3–4
20. a 2:4
21. c 1:5
22. b 2:22
23. a 3:1
24. a 3
25. b 2
26. c 2:2
27. d 3:4
28. a 1:8
29. c 2:5
30. b 2
31. b 2:1
32. c 3:4
33. a 1:3
34. a 1:20
35. d 2:4
36. b 1:21
37. a 2:12
38. c 1:9
39. a 1:20
40. b 1:10
41. b 2:18
42. c 2:1
43. a 2:1
44. b 2:22
45. d 1:21
46. c 1:1–17
47. c 2:16
48. a 1:9
49. c 2:22
50. c 1:20
51. a 2:14
52. c 2:1
53. a 2:11
54. c 1:10
55. d 1:14
56. a 2:1
57. c 1
58. d 1–2
59. a 1:15–16
60. d 2:11
61. a 2:12
62. b 2
63. d 1–2
64. d 28:20
65. b 2:7
66. c 1:23
67. a 2:13
68. a 2:22
69. d 1:3
70. c 1:1
71. b 1:18
72. c 1:24
73. b 3:4
74. a 2:16
75. d 1:19–20
76. d 1:1–16
77. b 1:17
78. a 2:22
79. a 2:11
80. c 2:2
81. c 4:1–11
82. c 2:17
83. a 1:14
84. d 2:21
85. a 1:5
86. a 2:22
87. d 1:16
88. b 1:18
89. c 1:10
90. c 1:20
91. c 2:10
92. d 2:22
93. a 1:15
94. b 2:8
95. a 1–2
96. c 1:21
97. b 1–2
98. d 1–2
99. a 2:2
100. a 1:16; 27:56, 61
101. d 1–2
102. a 3:3
103. b 1:12
104. c 1:23
105. d 1:16
106. c 2:13
107. c 1:9
108. d 1:18
109. a 1:20
110. b 1:23
111. d 1:1
112. c 1–2
113. a 3:6
114. a 2:22
115. c 1:15
116. a 2:3
117. c 2:22
118. b 2:12
119. b 2:19–23
120. a 2:11

121. a 2:17
122. c 1:1ff.
123. b 1:19
124. b 2:1–12
125. b 2:8
126. a 1:23
127. a 1:12
128. a 1:20
129. a 2:2
130. a 2:23
131. d 2:1
132. a 1:2
133. a 1:23
134. b 1:10
135. b 1:24
136. c 1:2
137. a 2:12
138. a 1:18–25
139. b 2:1
140. c 2:9
141. b 2:6
142. d 1–2

143. b 2:1
144. a 1:25
145. a 1:20
146. c 1:17
147. b 1:1–16
148. b 2:15
149. d 1:20
150. d 2:16
151. d 1:18
152. a 1:24
153. d 1:17
154. c 2:2
155. b 3:4
156. a 1:1
157. a 1:19
158. d 2:12
159. c 2:2
160. c 1:21
161. b 1:20
162. c 1:23
163. d 1–2

164. c 1:19
165. c 2:13
166. a 2:23
167. c 2:19
168. d 1–2
169. d 2:13
170. b 2:20
171. d 2:7–8
172. c 1:15–16
173. b 3:1
174. c 2:18
175. c 2:22
176. d 3:2
177. d 1:1
178. a 2:9
179. c 1:17
180. d 1:21
181. c 2:13
182. d 2:2
183. d 2:15
184. a 2:16

Chapter 2

1. c 4:18
2. b 4:18
3. b 4:21
4. d 5:13
5. a 8:26
6. d 9:10–11
7. a 16:18
8. d 10:1
9. d 16:18
10. b 14:28
11. a 10:2
12. d 10:16
13. c 14:19
14. a 14:29
15. a 9:9
16. b 8:23
17. c 4:18
18. a 4:21
19. d 10:4
20. c 9:9
21. b 8:14
22. b 16:13–18
23. a 12:1–2
24. d 14:25
25. b 5:14
26. d 8:14
27. b 9:9
28. a 4:18
29. d 4:18–22
30. b 5:1

31. b 4:21
32. b 10:2, 4
33. a 10:2–3
34. d 8:27
35. c 8:15
36. b 10:2–3
37. a 14:12
38. c 14:24
39. d 10:16
40. a 16:17
41. a 14:34
42. c 10:3
43. b 9:38
44. a 8:25
45. c 8:14
46. d 4:20
47. c 4:17
48. b 10:5
49. d 8:25
50. c 10:5
51. d 14:33
52. a 16:18–19
53. d 5:13
54. d 10:2–5
55. c 9:11
56. b 9:11
57. b 4:20
58. d 4:18
59. a 4:18
60. a 4:21

61. c 4:13
62. c 4:18
63. b 4–5
64. b 10:4
65. a 10:4
66. a 9:10
67. a 10:12
68. b 13:4–9
69. c 14:26
70. d 10:3
71. a 10:1
72. b 9:14
73. c 10:5
74. a 10:2
75. d 4:20
76. b 4:18
77. c 4:19
78. a 4:21
79. d 4:21
80. a 4:22
81. a 4:18
82. d 4:18
83. a 4:18
84. b 4–5
85. c 4:13
86. c 10:3
87. a 9:14
88. b 14:17
89. b 10:8
90. d 4:21

91. c 4:21
92. b 10:16
93. c 4:21
94. d 4:23

95. c 14:30–31
96. a 10:6
97. b 4:13

98. c 4:22
99. a 10:4
100. d 16:20

Chapter 3

1. c 3:15
2. a 4:18–19
3. b 5:4
4. a 13:23
5. a 5:10
6. b 13:44
7. c 13:32
8. b 13:25
9. a 25:14–30
10. a 13:44
11. b 5:3–12
12. c 20:16
13. b 20:8
14. c 25:6
15. d 13:32
16. b 4:23
17. d 13:37
18. d 13:6
19. b 13:27–28
20. c 13:33
21. d 22:3
22. d 13:33
23. a 3:1–17
24. c 4:4, 7, 10
25. c 5:3–12
26. d 5:7
27. a 13:3–4
28. a 21:30
29. b 13:30
30. c 13:6
31. a 25:13
32. c 13:16
33. b 5:1

34. c 25:17
35. b 13:48
36. b 13:4
37. c 5
38. d 13:22
39. b 13:31
40. c 3:15
41. d 5:3
42. d 13:8
43. c 5:8
44. a 13:33
45. c 13:25
46. a 13:32
47. a 25:5
48. b 13:38
49. a 13:36–43
50. b 21:31
51. c 25:2
52. d 13:38
53. b 22:2
54. d 5:11–12
55. c 25:14
56. d 13:30
57. a 13:32
58. a 4:4
59. c 4:19
60. a 5:5
61. c 13:2–3
62. d 13:19
63. a 5:11–12
64. a 13:30
65. d 13:33

66. d 25:1–13
67. b 21:33
67. b 21:33
68. c 13:4–23
69. b 13:39
70. c 5:5
71. d 5:1, 2, 14
72. d 20:1–16
73. d 25:28
74. a 20:12
75. c 18:35
76. c 18:22
77. b 3:15
78. c 4:10
79. d 4:4, 7, 10
80. d 4:12,17
81. c 13:20
82. d 5:1–2
83. c 5:3
84. d 13:26
85. c 13:24
86. d 5:9
87. c 13:49
88. c 22:14
89. d 4:4
90. a 4:7
91. c 13:7
92. b 5:6
93. d 3:14
94. c 25:13
95. a 21:28–29
96. c 25:15

Chapter 4

1. c 3:13–15
2. d 7:12
3. c 5:44
4. a 7:15
5. d 9:37
6. c 17:20
7. c 12:50
8. a 22:21
9. b 19:8
10. b 12:30
11. c 11:25

12. b 6:24
13. a 7:6
14. c 5:30
15. a 5:23–24
16. b 4:4
17. a 5:16
18. b 6:17
19. d 5:39
20. c 7:15
21. b 15:19
22. c 28:16–20

23. a 10:34
24. a 12:8
25. d 6:26
26. c 19:28
27. d 11:11
28. b 6:20
29. b 5:25
30. a 5:35
31. b 6:34
32. c 6:22
33. d 10:28

34. c 11:27
35. c 23:8
36. a 19:6
37. b 16:24
38. b 18:22
39. d 11:27
40. c 7:20
41. b 7:13–14
42. c 7:7
43. a 6:21
44. b 5:41
45. a 5:44
46. b 5:25
47. a 5:22
48. d 5:32
49. a 4:10
50. d 3:13–15
51. c 6:4
52. a 6:33
53. b 7:15–16
54. d 7:14

55. a 18:4
56. d 19:30
57. a 17:12
58. a 12:37
59. c 10:38
60. c 6:24
61. b 5:44–45
62. d 6:19
63. d 5:36–37
64. b 4:1–4
65. c 4:17
66. b 10:31
67. a 9:13
68. a 10:23
69. c 19:17
70. a 23:15
71. b 18:15
72. a 12:39
73. d 5:42
74. c 5:39

75. a 6:28–30
76. d 15:11
77. c 15:14
78. c 8:20
79. d 9:13
80. d 4:7
81. a 4:18–19
82. c 19:13–14
83. d 5:30
84. c 5:28
85. d 5:18
86. c 5:34–35
87. c 5:13
88. d 7:12
89. a 19:9
90. d 19:5
91. d 6:2
92. c 5:19
93. d 23:9
94. b 11:11

Chapter 5

1. a 1:18
2. b 8:14–15
3. d 15:21–28
4. c 28:16
5. b 9:34
6. d 27:32–34
7. a 17:14–21
8. d 1:18–20
9. c 8:1–4
10. b 27:53
11. b 14:22–23
12. d 9:27–30
13. a 17:1–2
14. a 9:20–22
15. c 28:16
16. a 15:21–28
17. d 1:18
18. d 4:1–3
19. d 8:1–4
20. c 8:4
21. d 28:1–3
22. c 1:20
23. a 9:20–22
24. b 28:7–9
25. d 20:29–34
26. a 3:13–17
27. d 15:21–28
28. b 8:14–15
29. d 12:9–14
30. b 8:1–3
31. d 3:16
32. c 12:9–13

33. d 1:18
34. a 17:14–18
35. b 28:1–6
36. a 8:28–32
37. d 9:18–25
38. a 8:1–4
39. b 8:1–3
40. c 28:2
41. b 14:13–21
42. a 8:1–4
43. b 9:27
44. d 8:5–13
45. b 4:23–24
46. d 28:16–20
47. b 2:4–6
48. c 1:18
49. c 28:2
50. b 15:21–28
51. d 1:20
52. d 1:23
53. c 8:23–27
54. d 4:23–24
55. a 28:2–3
56. a 15:39
57. c 1:19–20
58. a 8:14–15
59. d 15:21–22
60. b 9:20–22
61. d 27:53
62. c 9:2, 6, 7
63. c 9:29–30
64. d 8:5–13

65. d 8:5–13
66. b 1:20
67. a 8:1–2
68. c 15:32
69. a 8:5–7
70. c 17:14–21
71. d 4:24
72. c 8:28–32
73. b 12:9–13
74. d 28:1–20
75. d 27:11–26
76. c 1:23
77. b 8:5–7
78. c 20:29–34
79. a 28:2–6
80. c 8:14–15
81. b 8:5–13
82. b 1:19–20
83. a 28:1–6
84. c 27:54
85. c 8:4
86. a 12:9–14
87. d 28:2
88. b 15:22
89. d 3:16–17
90. a 14:13–21
91. d 27:54
92. c 9:23–25
93. d 9:32–33
94. c 9:20
95. d 8:28–32
96. d 1–2

Chapter 6

1. a 2:19–23
2. b 3:16
3. c 4:2
4. d 4:24
5. d 9:34
6. a 24:31
7. b 5:3
8. b 11:23
9. c 16:23
10. d 22:30
11. b 16:18
12. c 8:30–32
13. d 7:22
14. a 1:21–23
15. b 3:16
16. c 6:13
17. b 4:8–9
18. d 3:16
19. d 16:23
20. b 28:5–7
21. a 9:32–34
22. b 13:39
23. b 17:21
24. a 10:5–8
25. b 14:26
26. d 1:20
27. d 8:28
28. a 28:1–5
29. c 8:28
30. b 2:12–22
31. c 4:1–11
32. a 1:20–21
33. c 8:28
34. a 8:12
35. d 13:38–39
36. a 16:27
37. c 2:13, 20
38. a 17:18
39. b 10:1
40. b 8:28
41. a 1:20
42. d 3:11
43. b 4:23–24
44. d 4:5–6
45. c 4:1
46. d 12:31
47. a 8:32
48. c 26:41
49. a 15:21–22
50. a 10:6–8
51. d 16:21–23
52. b 1:18
53. a 13:39
54. c 8:16
55. b 8:32
56. a 2:19
57. a 3:13
58. c 26:41
59. a 4:3
60. c 4:9
61. b 3:13
62. c 10:18–20
63. b 12:43–45
64. d 25:41
65. a 12:18
66. c 17:19–20
67. a 2:13
68. a 12:26
69. d 27:50–52
70. c 16:23
71. a 16:23
72. c 1:20–21
73. d 1:19–20
74. a 3:11
75. a 4:11
76. d 4:2–3
77. a 4:1
78. d 1–2
79. c 5:22
80. d 2:13
81. d 24:36
82. d 18:10
83. a 5:29–30
84. c 12:24
85. d 17:14–16
86. c 4:6
87. d 24:36
88. d 13:42
89. b 8:28–29
90. d 27:50
91. c 12:24
92. b 10:25
93. d 13:49
94. b 8:28–32
95. b 24:31
96. b 4:5

Chapter 7

1. b 1:22–23
2. a 2:6
3. c 24:51
4. d 3:1–3
5. d 2:23
6. a 3:2–3
7. d 21:9
8. b 16:27
9. d 24:11
10. d 11:21–24
11. b 24:28
12. b 26:20–25
13. a 2:6
14. a 1:20
15. c 21:18–19
16. c 15:2, 7
17. c 1:22–23
18. a 2:5–6
19. b 24:35
20. a 5:17
21. b 2:16–18
22. d 8:17
23. c 11:14
24. b 13:35
25. a 24:9
26. a 26:31
27. d 24:29
28. d 4:7
29. b 8:11
30. b 21:9
31. c 24:6
32. d 4:7
33. d 2:23
34. c 2:3–5
35. a 2:23
36. a 4:4
37. b 21:9
38. a 16:21
39. d 12:21
40. a 4:17
41. b 1:23
42. c 4
43. b 2:15
44. d 21:13
45. b 4:4
46. a 2:18
47. c 4:6
48. d 1:23
49. c 24:29
50. d 1:20
51. b 4:15
52. c 6:25
53. b 28:20
54. a 24:30–31

55. c 2:15
56. b 2:5
57. b 1:20–21
58. d 16:3
59. a 24:15–16
60. a 21:9
61. c 3:2–3
62. c 1:22–23
63. a 24:36
64. d 25:33
65. c 2:16–18
66. a 4:13–16
67. b 3:3
68. a 24:1–2
69. c 24:14
70. b 21:13
71. d 2:18
72. c 11:11
73. d 24:44
74. b 2:16–18
75. c 16:22
76. a 24:7
77. b 24:22
78. a 24:37
79. a 1:22–23
80. c 1:23
81. d 2:5
82. c 1:23
83. a 25:33
84. b 8:17
85. c 2:5–6
86. a 1:22–23
87. c 1:20
88. a 4:10
89. d 24:3
90. b 24:15
91. c 17:12
92. b 15:8
93. c 4:4
94. d 24:7–8

Chapter 8

1. c 2:2
2. a 11:30
3. a 6:11
4. d 17:24–27
5. c 11:23
6. a 7:16
7. c 12:40
8. d 2:19–20
9. a 3:10
10. b 4:3
11. a 1:11
12. b 14:19
13. d 27:51–52
14. b 5:13
15. c 14:8–11
16. d 2:2
17. b 3:4
18. a 4:13
19. b 20:29–30
20. c 27:51–52
21. c 10:9
22. c 2:1
23. a 14:29
24. d 21:12
25. d 13:4
26. c 7:15
27. c 12:1
28. a 3:4
29. b 10:16
30. b 7:24
31. a 16:19
32. b 27:3–4
33. d 15:24
34. b 15:2
35. a 4:18
36. d 7:6
37. d 15:34–38
38. b 2:1
39. d 3:12
40. a 4:6
41. c 2:19–20
42. d 3:16
43. c 3:4
44. d 3:4
45. b 28:2
46. b 16:18
47. d 10:16
48. a 6:22
49. b 2:2
50. b 3:3
51. d 8:26
52. b 16:17–18
53. a 12:40
54. d 12:11–12
55. d 5:1
56. c 4:3
57. b 14:22–27
58. c 17:5
59. a 2:2
60. a 3:1
61. d 16:19
62. c 16:2
63. b 2:6
64. a 3:6
65. d 4:4
66. b 7:6
67. d 27:29
68. b 18:12
69. d 13:45–46
70. a 12:40
71. c 3:4
72. c 6:26
73. a 5:5
74. d 13:44
75. c 3:9
76. d 2:1–2
77. b 2:1
78. a 14:32
79. d 27:45
80. b 17:24–27
81. c 21:6–7

Chapter 9

1. d 26:3
2. b 26:7
3. c 26:20
4. a 26:18
5. b 26:36
6. b 26:45
7. a 26:47
8. b 26:65
9. d 26:49
10. d 26:69
11. a 27:2
12. b 27:19
13. c 27:24
14. b 27:60
15. c 27:54
16. d 27:47
17. c 27:28
18. a 27:32
19. a 27:34
20. b 26:64
21. d 26:50

22. b 27:9–10
23. d 27:20
24. c 26:37–38
25. b 26:28
26. d 26:25
27. c 26:4
28. c 26:15
29. d 26:17
30. d 27:15
31. c 27:6
32. b 26:73
33. d 26:65
34. c 26:60
35. d 26:51
36. d 27:55–56
37. c 27:50
38. b 27:30
39. a 27:25
40. b 27:45
41. b 26:17
42. c 26:14
43. c 26:29
44. d 26:40
45. a 26:48–49
46. b 26:21
47. a 27:8
48. d 26:74
49. b 27:18
50. b 26:58
51. b 26:56
52. a 27:48
53. d 27:26
54. c 27:27,29
55. b 27:29
56. c 27:59
57. b 27:52
58. d 27:7
59. a 27:11–26
60. a 26:69
61. d 26:18
62. b 26:5
63. c 26:15
64. b 26:24
65. c 26:39–44
66. c 26:37
67. a 26:30
68. a 26:26
69. c 27:33
70. b 27:5
71. d 26:63
72. b 26:53
73. c 26:75
74. d 26:73
75. a 27:60
76. d 27:31
77. c 27:46,50
78. a 27:49
79. b 26:71
80. d 27:15
81. b 26:2
82. a 26:6
83. a 26:26
84. b 26:24
85. d 26:35
86. c 26:32
87. a 27:54
88. a 27:29
89. d 27:24
90. a 27:34
91. a 27:61
92. c 27:51
93. a 27:53
94. b 26:39
95. c 26:30
96. a 26:15

Chapter 10

1. a 13:44
2. d 1–2
3. c 1:20–23
4. a 3:17
5. b 4:3,6
6. a 5:3,10,12
7. c 23:22
8. d 21:22
9. c 19:24
10. b 6:9,10
11. a 6:4
12. a 1:22–23
13. b 7:7
14. c 19:28
15. d 28:9
16. b 24:29
17. c 6:7
18. d 5:19
19. a 3:16–17
20. b 16:16–19
21. d 3:14–15
22. b 6:5
23. a 19:24
24. a 7:8
25. c 16:27
26. d 18:19
27. b 26:53
28. c 13:52
29. a 1:20
30. d 4:7,10
31. b 26:64
32. d 7:11
33. d 3:2
34. c 6:20
35. d 10:29
36. c 5:18
37. b 28:2
38. a 19:6
39. d 1–2
40. c 11:25
41. d 5:20
42. a 1:23
43. c 22:21
44. a 28:18
45. a 1:23
46. c 6:30
47. b 18:3
48. a 27:46
49. c 19:17
50. b 8:11
51. a 19:25–26
52. c 4:3
53. b 3:9
54. d 6:24
55. a 7:14
56. d 22:2
57. c 1:20
58. a 2:15
59. c 3:1–2
60. a 5:8
61. d 26:59–61
62. a 24:30
63. c 3:9
64. b 2:5–6
65. d 1–2
66. b 28:5
67. a 6:7
68. b 6:14
69. c 1:20
70. d 6:6
71. a 3:16–17
72. c 27:46
73. b 13:24
74. d 12:50
75. a 6:24
76. a 21:13
77. d 19:21
78. b 1:20,24
79. d 1–2
80. b 19:23
81. c 18:10

82. d 13:47–50
83. d 23:9
84. a 13:33
85. a 13:10–13

86. b 18:20
87. b 6:18
88. d 25:31
89. a 22:37–38

90. a 13:10–11
91. d 6:33
92. d 23:13
93. b 5:34

General Questions

History/Archaeology

1. b	12. a	23. c
2. b	13. b	24. c
3. a	14. c	25. a
4. b	15. b	26. b
5. c	16. a	27. c
6. b	17. c	28. b
7. c	18. c	29. c
8. c	19. c	30. d
9. c	20. a	31. a
10. c	21. c	32. d
11. d	22. c	33. b

Unique/Features

1. a	13. c	24. b
2. d	14. d	25. a
3. b	15. a	26. b
4. a	16. b	27. d
5. a	17. d	28. a
6. b	18. a	29. b
7. c	19. d	30. d
8. d	20. b	31. b
9. a	21. d	32. b
10. a	22. c	33. c
11. a	23. b	34. d
12. b		

Geography

1. b	12. a	23. b
2. a	13. c	24. d
3. c	14. c	25. b
4. b	15. d	26. b
5. c	16. b	27. d
6. a	17. b	28. b
7. b	18. d	29. d
8. d	19. b	30. c
9. a	20. a	31. c
10. d	21. b	32. c
11. d	22. c	33. d